Kids on the Go

KIDS ON THE GO
Activity Logs for Young Travelers

John Haberberger

1994
TEACHER IDEAS PRESS
A Division of
Libraries Unlimited, Inc.
Englewood, Colorado

I want to thank my family for their interest and support in this endeavor. Thanks also to Sue Conley and Mike Fitzgerald for their enthusiasm, encouragement, and knowledge, which made my task much easier, and thanks to Nancy Dye for the help she gave me in the beginning.

This book is dedicated to all the children I've had the pleasure to know. I have learned a great deal from you, and you have made teaching a rewarding career for me.

TEACHER IDEAS PRESS
A Division of
Libraries Unlimited, Inc.
P.O. Box 6633
Englewood, CO 80155-6633
1-800-237-6124

Library of Congress Cataloging-in-Publication Data

Haberberger, John.
    Kids on the go : activity logs for young travelers / John Haberberger.
        xiv, 115 p. 22x28 cm.
        ISBN 1-56308-058-3
        1. Children--Travel--United States--Study and teaching--Activity programs. 2. United States--Geography--Study and teaching--Activity programs. 3. Children--Travel--Study and teaching--Activity programs. I. Title.
    E158.H17 1994
    917.3'0076--dc20   93-39049
                                                                           CIP

Contents

STATES AND CITIES

FOREIGN TRAVEL

WAYS TO TRAVEL

FIELD TRIPS

Introduction

The challenges facing the education profession are far greater today in our rapidly changing world than in years past. We are required to meet the academic and socioemotional needs of a much more diverse population of youngsters. It is important for us to teach children not only basic skills to function in today's complex society, but also how to use those skills—how to think and solve problems.

Every teacher is used to hearing the words, "We will be taking Johnny out of school for a week. His father has business in Florida. Would you please get some work ready for him to take along," or something similar. When this has happened to me I have weighed carefully the benefits of tearing out workbook pages to send along. It seemed to me that there must be something more relevant, something that would allow the child to become an active learner while away from the classroom, and something that would encourage parents to work with their children.

So I prepared mini-travel booklets for the vacationing child. These booklets included questions on the type of transportation used to reach the destination and questions focusing on the place visited. *Kids on the Go* is based on these original booklets.

Being an educator I know the importance of helping students develop higher levels of thinking. I therefore used Bloom's Taxonomy as a guide in preparing my traveling curricula. I attempt to pose questions and activities that draw from different levels of the taxonomy.

Kids on the Go is intended for use in the elementary school. The teacher need only copy the appropriate pages for a particular trip, but I would recommend that the assignment be tailored to each child. The How to Use This Book section will give you some ideas for this.

I have been successful using this approach for students who miss school work while traveling. Students are required to use the skills they learned in the classroom as they broaden their knowledge base. Students and parents have responded favorably to this idea. I have enjoyed preparing this tool and I hope you enjoy using it.

How to Use This Book

Teachers, here are some ideas to help you when you use *Kids on the Go* with your students.

1. It is important to tailor the assignments to the ability level of the child. Some questions and activities are too difficult for some and too easy for others, so you can guide the child in choosing those that are appropriate for him or her. You also need to fill in the number of questions or activities at the top of the pages. It would be helpful to go over the assignment with the child and the parents first and answer any questions they might have.

2. In some of the questions and activities the child is asked to make comparisons. To facilitate this I have included a Venn diagram in appendix B. You can make a copy of the diagram for the child.

3. In appendix A is a listing of the states, with the capital city, date of statehood, and various state symbols. This is for your information to use as needed.

4. The questions and activities for field trips are to use after a field trip, either in class or as follow-up homework. If a traveling student is visiting an art museum or a historical museum, the relevant field trip pages could be additional or alternative assignments.

5. The foreign travel questions and activities are generic. You may want to make these site-specific to the destination of the child.

6. Students should be given the option of keeping a diary or journal of their travels. They also could prepare a scrapbook or photo journal to share with the class. These options could be in addition to other activities or could replace them.

7. In some activities the children are asked to make a model. I would not expect this to be done while traveling but rather at home when they return.

8. The pages of *Kids on the Go* are intended to be copied for the students. Answers should be written on separate paper. You can decide the manner in which the child will present it to you.

9. I have provided you with a basic framework to broaden the knowledge base of the child leaving your classroom. Because of space limitations I have likely omitted things you deem important. Feel free to expand upon these materials and to use them in the way that best suits your situation.

Letter to Parents

When you send home the travel booklet for a child's trip, a letter should be included. The following is one that can be modified as appropriate.

Dear [Name of Parent],

Your child leaving class to accompany you provides an excellent opportunity to learn the geography and special attractions of [specify state or region or foreign country]. The questions and activities in the enclosed booklet are meant to enhance your child's learning experience. I would like you to use the booklet as a replacement for homework or as a supplement to other work I have assigned. The questions and activities are designed to allow your child to be an active learner and thinker while traveling. I encourage you to assist your child as needed.

Sincerely,

STATES AND CITIES

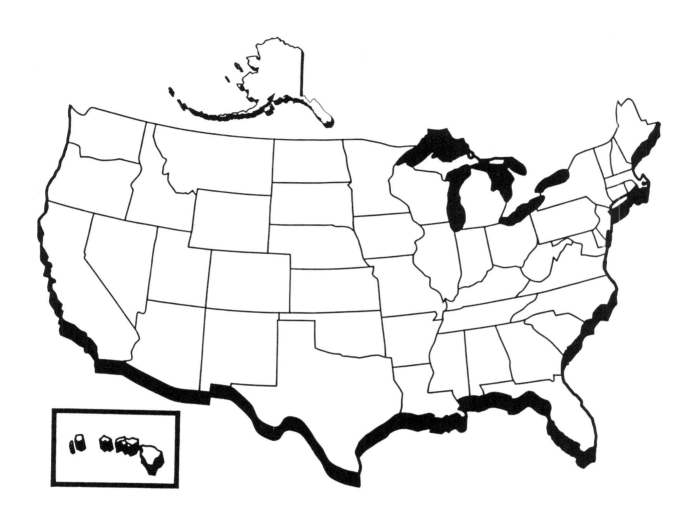

ALABAMA

Parents, have your child complete
___ questions and ___ activities.

Questions

1. Name the capital city of Alabama.

2. Alabama's nickname is Heart of Dixie. What is the origin of the word *Dixie*? Explain the meaning of the nickname. Is it geographically accurate?

3. Name the states that border Alabama.

4. In 1861 Alabama became the fourth state to secede from the Union. What does *secede* mean? Write a report explaining why Alabama seceded.

5. Tuscumbia is the birthplace of Helen Keller. Who was Helen Keller and why was she a famous person?

6. In Cullman is the Ave Maria Grotto. Who was the Benedictine monk who built the miniature replicas of the famous churches? If you visited the grotto, write a one-paragraph description of a church you saw and draw a picture of it.

7. The George C. Marshall Space Flight Center is found in Huntsville. If you visited the center, write about the things you saw and did. Why is space exploration important?

8. In Montgomery is the nation's first Civil Rights memorial. Explain the meaning of the term *civil rights*. Explain why the memorial was built. Who designed the memorial?

9. Mobile celebrates Mardi Gras in February or early March, depending on when the Lenten Season begins each year. If you went to the Mardi Gras, write about the things you saw and did.

Activities

1. Draw a map that shows where the Mason-Dixon line is. What was the importance of that line?

2. Read a biography of Helen Keller and prepare a report to share what you learned with the class when you return.

3. If you visited the Ave Maria Grotto and saw the miniature replicas, build a miniature or draw a picture of one of the replicas.

4. If you visited the Space Flight Center, prepare a report on what you saw and did. You could also build a model rocket and explain how a rocket engine works.

5. Design a spacecraft of your own and draw a picture of it. Explain the different features of your craft.

6. If you saw the Civil Rights memorial draw a picture of it.

From *Kids on the Go* by John Haberberger • ©1994 • Teacher Ideas Press • P.O. Box 6633 • Englewood, CO 80155-6633

ALASKA

Parents, have your child complete ___ questions and ___ activities.

Questions

1. Name the capital city of Alaska.

2. Name the largest city in the state.

3. In what year did Alaska become a state? How many years has it been a state?

4. The name *Alaska* comes from an Aleut word, *alakshak*. What is the meaning of the word?

5. Alaska has an unofficial state nickname, Last Frontier. What is a frontier? Why is Alaska the Last Frontier? Write about another last frontier.

6. Name the two mountain systems found in Alaska.

7. Mount McKinley, the highest mountain in North America, is in Alaska. The mountain is also called *Denali*, a Tanana Indian name. What does the word *Denali* mean? How high is the mountain?

8. The Arctic region of Alaska has twenty-four hours of sunshine in the summer but no direct sunlight from mid-November to mid-January. Explain this phenomenon.

9. Alaska has many glaciers. What is a glacier? How fast do glaciers move? What effects do they have on the earth?

Activities

1. Draw a picture of the Alaska state flag. Who had the idea for the state flag?

2. Draw a map of Alaska. Your map should include major cities, the two mountain systems, Mount McKinley (Denali) National Park, the Arctic Ocean, the Bering Sea, the Pacific Ocean, and the Alaska Pipeline.

3. The fiftieth anniversary of the Alaska Highway, the road that connects Alaska with the lower forty-eight states, was celebrated in 1992. The highway begins in Dawson Creek, British Columbia (Canada), and ends in Fairbanks, Alaska. Plan a vacation for your family traveling on this road. Allow about two weeks—this is not a freeway. Plan where you will stop each night and what you will do on the way. Have fun!

4. In Alaska you are able to see the northern lights or aurora borealis. Explain what causes this phenomenon. Draw a picture of the lights if you saw them. Explain the Eskimo legend of the northern lights.

From *Kids on the Go* by John Haberberger • ©1994 • Teacher Ideas Press • P.O. Box 6633 • Englewood, CO 80155-6633

ARIZONA

Parents, have your child complete
___ questions and ___ activities.

Questions

1. Name the capital city of Arizona.

2. Arizona is a western state. Name the states that border Arizona.

3. The Grand Canyon, in Arizona, is one of the seven natural wonders of the world. Name the river that flows through the canyon. Explain how the canyon was formed.

4. Arizona has twenty-three Indian reservations with a Native American population larger than that of any other state. Name the largest tribe in Arizona and write a report about the tribe's culture.

5. Near Phoenix are the Superstition Mountains. For many years prospectors have searched these mountains for the Lost Dutchman Mine. Explain the legend of the Lost Dutchman Mine. This mine has never been found and some say that it is a myth. What is a myth?

6. The Petrified Forest National Park, near Holbrook, has the most spectacular display of petrified wood in the world. What is petrified wood?

Activities

1. Design a license plate using the Grand Canyon State nickname. Draw a picture of your idea.

2. Show pictures or actual examples of the various crafts of the Navajo. These include basketry, pottery, rugs, jewelry, and Kachina dolls.

3. If you saw the Grand Canyon, draw a picture of a portion of it that you saw.

4. Draw a map of the Superstition Mountains. On your map include the Lost Dutchman Mine. Using clues left by the man who found the mine, indicate where you think it is.

5. Prepare a report on petrified wood. Draw a flowchart showing the steps that occur in the process.

6. Draw pictures of the different varieties of cactus that are found in Arizona. Explain how a cactus could help you if you were in the desert without water.

ARKANSAS

Parents, have your child complete
___ questions and ___ activities.

Questions

1. What does the word *Arkansas* mean? From which Native American language does it come?

2. Name the six states that border Arkansas.

3. Name the capital city of Arkansas.

4. Arkansas is called the Land of Opportunity and the Natural State. Explain why it has these two nicknames.

5. The first permanent settlement in Arkansas was a trading post. Give the name of this post and the name of the man who established it.

6. Timber is an important industry in Arkansas. Name ten tree varieties that grow in the state. Name five things that are made from wood. Name five animals that depend on trees for their homes.

7. Near Murfreesboro is the Crater of Diamonds State Park, the only North American diamond mine open to the public. Here visitors may dig for diamonds and keep what they find. Name the other precious stones that are found in this park.

Activities

1. Design a license plate using either the Land of Opportunity or the Natural State nickname.

2. If you visited Arkansas Post National Memorial prepare a report on what you saw there. Build a model of the Spanish fort found there.

3. Hot Springs National Park is one of the most popular spas and resorts in the United States. Prepare a report on this park. Tell what thermal water is and where it comes from. Explain why people visit the Physical Medicine Center for hydrotherapy treatments.

4. If you visited the Crater of Diamonds State Park, prepare a report on what you saw. Explain how to dig for diamonds. If you found a diamond, show it to the class when you return.

5. Draw a map of Arkansas. Your map should include major cities, the Ozark and Ouachita mountain ranges, the Arkansas River, and the Mississippi River.

From *Kids on the Go* by John Haberberger • ©1994 • Teacher Ideas Press • P.O. Box 6633 • Englewood, CO 80155-6633

CALIFORNIA

Parents, have your child complete
___ questions and ___ activities.

Questions

1. California is a western state. Which states border California? California is next to which ocean?

2. What is the capital city of California?

3. California is called the Golden State. Explain why it has this nickname.

4. The elevation of California ranges from 282 feet below sea level to 14,494 feet above. What place is below sea level? What is the highest point in the state?

5. The oldest trees in the world are found in California. Give the name of these trees and tell how old they are.

6. California leads the nation in the production of more than thirty- five fruits and vegetables. Name some fruits and vegetables that are grown in California.

7. The discovery of gold in 1849 may have been the most important event in the history of California. Explain how this event changed California.

Activities

1. Draw a map of California. Include major cities, Yosemite National Park, and the highest and lowest points in the state.

2. California has the oldest trees in the world. Make a list of ten of the oldest things you can think of. Brainstorm with your family to get ideas.

3. Eat a fruit or vegetable from California that you have never had before. Draw a picture of it and write a one-paragraph description of it. Tell how it tasted, smelled, felt, and looked. Did you like it?

4. Earthquakes occur often in California. Prepare a report on earthquakes and explain why California has so many.

5. Imagine that you work for the tourism industry of California and design a travel brochure for visitors to the state. Make a copy of your brochure.

6. Smog is a problem in California, as well as other places. What is smog? Brainstorm with your family and make a list of ways to eliminate smog and clean up the air.

LOS ANGELES, CALIFORNIA

Parents, have your child complete
___ questions and ___ activities.

Questions

1. In 1781 the Governor of California named the city that is now called Los Angeles. What was the original name he gave the town?

2. Los Angeles is next to which ocean?

3. Los Angeles, with its suburbs, is like a giant jigsaw puzzle. Write ten suburbs in alphabetical order. Los Angeles is spread out over how many square miles? How many people live in Los Angeles? Why is it important to own a car in Los Angeles?

4. In Los Angeles are many broadcasting stations. You can go on tours of CBS, ABC, and NBC. Tours of the Universal and Paramount movie studios are also available. If you went on any of these tours, write about what you saw and include one new thing you learned about television or the movies.

5. The historic ship *Queen Mary* is docked at Long Beach. If you took a tour of the ship, write about what you saw and learned. Would you like to take a voyage on an ocean liner? Write why or why not.

6. In Long Beach you will also find the *Spruce Goose*, a huge airplane built by Howard Hughes. Why is it called *Spruce Goose*? How big is the plane?

7. There are miles of beaches in the Los Angeles area. If you went to a beach, write about what you saw and did there. If this was your first time to see the ocean, describe the feelings you had.

Activities

1. Disneyland and Knott's Berry Farm has many rides and attractions. Create a new ride for either and draw a picture of your ride and explain how it works.

2. Become a movie director and make your own home movie about your trip to Los Angeles. Share it with the class when you return.

3. Draw a picture or build a model of the *Queen Mary*.

4. Draw a picture of the *Spruce Goose*.

5. Building sand castles is a popular activity at the beach. Use your imagination and think of something unusual to build out of sand at the beach. Draw a picture of your idea.

SAN DIEGO, CALIFORNIA

Parents, have your child complete
___ questions and ___ activities.

Questions

1. San Diego is "the place where California began." Give the name of the Portuguese conquistador who landed there in 1542.

2. San Diego is next to which ocean? If you went to the beach, write about what you saw and did there.

3. The San Diego Wild Animal Park is a preservation area for endangered species. What does *endangered* mean? Name five endangered animals. If you visited the park, write about one new thing that you learned.

4. From mid-December to mid-February, California gray whales migrate south from Alaska's Bering Sea to Baja California. They pass only a mile or so off the San Diego shoreline. What does *migrate* mean? Did you see the whales? How many were visible? Interview someone who has seen the whales regularly and write a report of your findings.

Activities

1. San Diego began as a mission in 1769. Draw a picture of the mission. Who established this mission?

2. San Diego has a Mexican flavor because it is close to Mexico. Name some of the Mexican things you saw there (such as clothing, jewelry, and pottery) and draw pictures of them.

3. Sea World is a popular attraction in San Diego. If you went there, what was your favorite show or exhibit? Design a Sea World T-shirt.

4. If you saw the whales as they went by, draw a picture of what you saw.

5. The San Diego Zoo is considered to be the best in the world. If you went to this zoo, draw a picture of an animal in its natural setting. Do you think that zoos are important? Write why or why not.

SAN FRANCISCO, CALIFORNIA

Parents, have your child complete
___ questions and ___ activities.

Questions

1. What was the original name of San Francisco?

2. San Francisco was built on forty-three hills. What is the elevation of San Francisco?

3. What historic event in 1849 resulted in many people coming to San Francisco?

4. San Francisco is a city of many apartment houses. Why do you think there are so many?

5. San Francisco is famous for its cable cars. If you rode one write about where you went and describe the ride. Compare a cable car with a train. Using the Venn diagram, show how they are alike and different.

6. The Golden Gate Bridge is a famous landmark in San Francisco. Why is it called the Golden Gate Bridge? What color is it painted?

7. San Francisco's Chinatown is the largest Chinese community outside of Asia. Why do you think so many Chinese choose to live in San Francisco?

8. Alcatraz Island is visible in the bay. What does the word *Alcatraz* mean? What is on the island? Explain why a prisoner would have a difficult time escaping from Alcatraz.

Activities

1. Draw a picture or build a model of a cable car.

2. Who are some well-known former inmates at Alcatraz? Draw a wanted poster for one of those criminals.

3. If you went to the Japan Center, write about what you learned about the Japanese culture. If you learned origami, the art of paper folding, demonstrate what you can do and teach the class to make something when you return.

4. San Francisco has a professional baseball team, the Giants, and a professional football team, the 49ers. Design a jersey for either team.

From *Kids on the Go* by John Haberberger • ©1994 • Teacher Ideas Press • P.O. Box 6633 • Englewood, CO 80155-6633

COLORADO

Parents, have your child complete
___ questions and ___ activities.

Questions

1. What is the capital city of Colorado?

2. Why is Colorado called the Centennial State? What does *centennial* mean? What does the word *Colorado* mean in Spanish?

3. Colorado is the highest state in the Union. Name the mountain range that runs through the state. Name the highest peak and give its height.

4. Pike's Peak is near Colorado Springs. For whom is this peak named? What is the height of Pike's Peak?

5. Tourism is an important industry in Colorado and skiing is popular in winter. If you went skiing in Colorado, name the area where you skied and tell what city it is near.

6. The Black Canyon of the Gunnison National Monument is found near Montrose. Why is it called the Black Canyon of the Gunnison?

7. Explain why Central City is an important historical landmark in Colorado.

8. The Great Sand Dunes National Monument near Alamosa has the tallest sand dunes in North America. Explain how these dunes were formed. If you visited the dunes, write about what you did there.

9. Mesa Verde National Park is famous for cliff dwellings in the canyon walls. What does *Mesa Verde* mean? Prepare a report about the dwellings and the Native Americans who lived there.

Activities

1. Design a license plate for Colorado.

2. Prepare a report on the Black Canyon. Tell how it was formed, how deep it is, and other facts that you learned.

3. Design and build a car to compete in the race up Pike's Peak.

4. Make a map of Colorado. Your map should include major cities, the Rocky Mountains, Pike's Peak, Rocky Mountain National Park, Mesa Verde National Park, and the Colorado River.

5. If you visited the Air Force Academy in Colorado Springs, draw a picture of the chapel you saw. Did you see any cadets? Draw a cadet in uniform.

From *Kids on the Go* by John Haberberger • ©1994 • Teacher Ideas Press • P.O. Box 6633 • Englewood, CO 80155-6633

DENVER, COLORADO

Parents, have your child complete
___ questions and ___ activities.

Questions

1. Denver is called the Mile High City. Name the point in the city that is exactly a mile high.

2. One of the U.S. Mint facilities is located in Denver. What is produced in a mint?

3. Larimer Street was the first street in Denver. If you visited Larimer Square, write about what you saw there.

4. Red Rocks Park is a natural amphitheater found west of Denver. What causes the rocks to be red in color? What is an amphitheater?

5. The Cherry Blossom Festival takes place in June at Sakura Square. If you went to this festival, write about the different things that you saw.

6. The National Western Stock Show and Rodeo is held in January in Denver. What is a rodeo? If you attended this show, write about the things that you saw and did.

7. Did you see the state capitol building? The granite dome is covered with what? How many steps are there to the top of the dome?

8. Denver has a large Hispanic population. Who are the Hispanic people? What is the importance of the annual Cinco de Mayo celebration?

Activities

1. If you took a tour of the U.S. Mint, prepare a report about the making of bills and coins. Tell whose picture is on these bills: one-dollar, five-dollar, ten-dollar, twenty-dollar and fifty-dollar.

2. Draw a picture of Larimer Square showing the facades of the early buildings in Denver.

3. Construct a Japanese kite, and when you return, teach the class the Japanese art of origami, show classmates how to use chopsticks, or tell about something else you learned from the Cherry Blossom Festival and Sakura Square.

4. Draw a picture of the Red Rocks amphitheater. Summer concerts are scheduled there each year with many popular artists performing. If you were attending a concert at Red Rocks, who would you like to see?

6. Imagine that you work for the U.S. Mint and are given the job of creating a new one-dollar bill. Draw a picture of what your new bill would look like. Whose picture would you choose to put on it?

7. Make a photo scrapbook of your visit to Denver and share it with the class when you return.

From *Kids on the Go* by John Haberberger • ©1994 • Teacher Ideas Press • P.O. Box 6633 • Englewood, CO 80155-6633

CONNECTICUT

Parents, have your child complete
___ questions and ___ activities.

Questions

1. Name the capital city of Connecticut.

2. Connecticut was the fifth of the original thirteen states. On what date did Connecticut enter the Union? How long has Connecticut been a state?

3. Explain why Connecticut is called the Constitution State.

4. In Hartford a plaque on Charter Oak Avenue marks the spot where the Charter Oak, a hollow tree, once stood. Explain the historical importance of the Charter Oak. What was hidden in the tree?

5. Bridgeport's most famous resident was probably P. T. Barnum, who ran the Greatest Show on Earth, a circus. Have you ever been to a circus? What was your favorite act? Would you want to be in a circus? If so, what would you like to do?

6. Groton is the home of a huge U.S. naval submarine base and is also where the first nuclear-powered submarine was built. What is the name of that submarine?

Activities

1. Draw a map of Connecticut. Your map should include major cities, the Atlantic Ocean, the Connecticut River, Long Island Sound, Groton, Hartford, and Bridgeport.

2. The state bird is the American robin. Design a license plate using that bird as a theme.

3. Design a T-shirt that advertises the Greatest Show on Earth.

4. Bridgeport had another famous resident, Charles S. Stratton, who was only twenty-eight inches tall. He was promoted by P. T. Barnum as General Tom Thumb. Draw a picture of Tom Thumb, using a ruler to measure the twenty-eight inches. Dress him in clothes he might have worn in the circus.

5. If you toured the submarine at Groton, tell about what you saw and learned. Draw a picture of the submarine. If you were able to go inside, how did it make you feel? Do you think that you could live underwater in a sub for long periods of time? Explain how a submarine works. How is it able to go underwater and come to the surface again? Build a model of a submarine.

From *Kids on the Go* by John Haberberger • ©1994 • Teacher Ideas Press • P.O. Box 6633 • Englewood, CO 80155-6633

DELAWARE

Parents, have your child complete
___ questions and ___ activities.

Questions

1. Name the capital city of Delaware.

2. Name the largest city in the state.

3. Delaware is next to Delaware Bay. For whom are the state and the bay named?

4. The first permanent settlement of Swedes in North America was in Delaware. Give the name of that settlement.

5. Delaware was the first state to adopt the Constitution of the United States. In what year did Delaware adopt it. What is the Constitution?

6. Delaware is called First State, Small Wonder, Diamond State, and Blue Hen State. Explain the meanings of these nicknames.

7. The Delaware state bird is the blue hen chicken. Explain why this bird was chosen. Draw a picture of the chicken.

Activities

1. The Fort Christina Monument, in Wilmington, was a gift from the people of Sweden. If you saw the monument, draw a picture of it.

2. Design a license plate using one of the four nicknames: First State, Small Wonder, Diamond State, or Blue Hen State.

3. Do you like to eat chicken? Write the recipe for your favorite chicken dish.

4. Draw a map of Delaware. Your map should include major cities, the Delaware River with Pea Patch Island, the Great Sand Hill, and the site of the first log cabin in northern Delaware.

5. Keep a diary or journal of your travels in Delaware, or make a photo scrapbook of your trip.

6. Pea Patch Island is an unusual name. Write a short, one-page story explaining how the island got its name.

FLORIDA

Parents, have your child complete
___ questions and ___ activities.

Questions

1. Name the states, the ocean, and the gulf that border Florida.

2. Name the first explorer who came to Florida.

3. Name the capital city of Florida.

4. Why is Florida called the Sunshine State?

5. Why is the city of St. Augustine an important historical site?

6. Florida leads the nation in the production of citrus fruits. Name three citrus fruits grown in Florida.

7. Everglades National Park is found near Miami. This is the largest subtropical wilderness in North America. Name some of the animals that live in the Everglades. What is the difference between a crocodile and an alligator? Draw a picture of each.

8. Walt Disney World has three major parks: The Magic Kingdom, Epcot Center, and Disney-MGM Studios. If you visited any of these, write about what you saw and did.

Activities

1. Design a license plate using the Sunshine State nickname.

2. Draw a map of Florida. Your map should include major cities, the Everglades, Lake Okeechobee, the Kennedy Space Center at Cape Canaveral, the Florida Keys, and St. Augustine.

3. The Orange Julius is a popular drink. When you get home, use a citrus fruit and other ingredients to create a new drink. Write the recipe for your drink. Make your new drink. How does it taste? Share it with the class.

4. Orlando has a Ripley's Believe It or Not! museum that is built like it is sinking into a hole. Who was Ripley? If you went to the museum, you saw some unusual things. Plan your own believe it or not museum. What oddities will you put in yours?

5. The Kennedy Space Center has been the launch site for all U.S. manned space missions since 1968. If you went there, write about what you saw. Build a rocket model to share with the class.

6. Walt Disney World has three major parks: The Magic Kingdom, Epcot Center, and Disney-MGM Studios. If you went there, do one of these activities: create a new "land" for the Magic Kingdom, design a car for the future, or make a movie of your Florida vacation.

ORLANDO, FLORIDA

Parents, have your child complete
___ questions and ___ activities.

Questions

1. Why is Orlando so popular with winter visitors?

2. Sea World of Florida is in Orlando. If you visited Sea World, write about the things you saw there.

3. Near Orlando is the Kennedy Space Center, which is the launch site for all U.S. manned space flights. Would you want to be an astronaut? Write your answer and explain your reason. If you went to Spaceport USA visitors center, write about the things you saw and include one new thing you learned.

4. If you visited Universal Studios Florida, you may have learned about special effects in movies. Write about the effect you found the most interesting. If you watched a production of "Nickelodeon," write about what you saw.

5. Walt Disney World has three major parks. Which park is your favorite? Write your answer and explain why.

6. At Epcot is the World Showcase. Write a list of the nations shown. If you could choose another nation in which to live, which one would it be? Write your answer and explain why.

Activities

1. Make a travel brochure for Orlando.

2. Using the Venn diagram, compare a whale and a dolphin. Show how they are alike and different. Draw pictures of the two animals.

3. A number of unmanned spacecraft are launched from the Kennedy Space Center. Prepare a report on these unmanned craft. Tell about the different satellites and other things sent into space and what their functions are.

4. If you saw a space shuttle or a rocket, draw a picture of it.

5. When you get home, make a model of a rocket.

6. Design a Disney World T-shirt.

7. Plan a birthday party for yourself at Disney World. Write a list of your guests, compose the invitation, and explain what you will do on that day.

GEORGIA

Parents, have your child complete
___ questions and ___ activities.

Questions

1. Name the capital city of Georgia.

2. Explain why Georgia is called the Peach State.

3. The Girl Guides, later called the Girl Scouts, was started in 1912 in Savannah. Name the woman who started this organization.

4. Name the man who founded the Georgia colony and tell for whom Georgia is named.

5. Georgia is a land of many firsts. One of these is the invention of the cotton gin by Eli Whitney in 1793. What did this machine do and why was it important to the cotton industry?

6. The Okefenokee Swamp is one of the largest preserved freshwater wetlands in the United States. Name some of the animals found there. The Creek Indians called it "land of trembling earth." Explain why the Creeks gave it that name.

7. In Stone Mountain Park is Memorial Hall, a Civil War museum. If you visited the museum, write about what you saw and learned about the Civil War.

Activities

1. Design a license plate for Georgia.

2. The Okefenokee Swamp floor has been described as "the most beautiful landscape in the world." If you visited the swamp, draw a picture of it and its floor, or make a diorama of the swamp. Your drawing or diorama should show the trees and aquatic flowers found in the swamp.

3. The Okefenokee Swamp Park has a serpentarium. If you visited this attraction, draw pictures of the serpents you saw there.

4. Stone Mountain Park, outside of Atlanta, contains the world's largest granite monolith. A monument to the Confederacy, the carving on the mountain's face depicts three men. Name them and draw a picture of the mountain showing the carved figures.

5. Georgia's state fruit is the peach. Write the recipe for a peach treat that you like, or create your own special peach dessert. You could make it and share it with the class when you return.

6. Keep a diary or journal of your travels in Georgia, or make a photo scrapbook of your trip.

From *Kids on the Go* by John Haberberger • ©1994 • Teacher Ideas Press • P.O. Box 6633 • Englewood, CO 80155-6633

ATLANTA, GEORGIA

Parents, have your child complete
___ questions and ___ activities.

Questions

1. The Creek Indians built a settlement on the original site of Atlanta. Write the name of that settlement.

2. In what year did Atlanta become the state capital of Georgia?

3. A popular soft drink was introduced in Atlanta. Write the name of the drink and the pharmacy where it was first served. What was the date?

4. Martin Luther King, Jr. was born in Atlanta. Who was Dr. King? Write a paragraph explaining why he was an important man.

5. The Museum of the Jimmy Carter Library is in Atlanta. The museum contains a replica of the Oval Office. Who uses the Oval Office and where is it found?

6. If you visited Underground Atlanta, write about the things you saw and did. Explain how this underground was created.

7. Stone Mountain Park contains the world's largest granite monolith. How high is it? What is a monolith? Write the names of the three men whose figures are carved on the face of the mountain. Explain their importance to the Confederacy.

Activities

1. Fox Theatre, one of the most lavish movie theaters in the world, is in Atlanta. If you visited the Fox, draw pictures of the different things you saw.

2. Pushcart peddlers are found in Underground Atlanta. Imagine that you have a pushcart. What things do you sell? Create an ad for your cart and product. Draw a picture of your idea.

3. Do you like Coca Cola? Be creative and invent a new soft drink. Write a list of the ingredients. What flavor is your drink?

4. If you visited Stone Mountain Park, draw a picture of the mountain showing the carving.

5. Prepare a report on Stone Mountain and the different things surrounding the mountain sculpture.

6. The Cable News Network (CNN) studio is in Atlanta. If you took a tour of the studio, prepare a report on what you saw and learned.

7. Imagine that you are a newscaster and prepare a news report. Your news could be national, local, or about your school or family.

8. If you visited the Jimmy Carter Library museum, draw a picture of the Oval Office.

From *Kids on the Go* by John Haberberger • ©1994 • Teacher Ideas Press • P.O. Box 6633 • Englewood, CO 80155-6633

HAWAII

Parents, have your child complete
___ questions and ___ activities.

Questions

1. Name the capital city of Hawaii. On which island is it found?

2. Name the Big Four islands in the Hawaiian Islands chain.

3. Hawaii, the first island state, became our fiftieth state on what date? How many years has Hawaii been a state?

4. What is the origin of the name *Hawaii*?

5. The state nickname is the Aloha State. What does *aloha* mean? What is aloha spirit?

6. Pearl Harbor, on the island of Oahu, is a U.S. naval base. If you took a tour of the base, write about the things you saw and did. What famous historical event happened at Pearl Harbor on December 7, 1941?

7. On the island of Maui is the Haleakala National Park. Haleakala is a volcano that has not erupted since 1790. You can go to the top for a spectacular view of the surrounding area, and you can also walk into the huge crater. If you walked into the crater, describe what you saw. Draw a picture of the inside of the crater. What does the word *Haleakala* mean?

Activities

1. Draw a picture of the Hawaii state flag.

2. Diamond Head, a long-extinct volcano, has long been Hawaii's trademark. Draw a picture of Diamond Head.

3. Draw a map of Hawaii. Your map should include Oahu, Hawaii (the Big Island), Maui, and Kauai. Your map should also show Pearl Harbor, Hawaii Volcanoes National Park, Diamond Head, and major cities.

4. The Hawaiian Islands are of volcanic origin. What is a volcano? What causes a volcano to erupt? Draw a picture of a volcano erupting.

5. As you traveled around Hawaii did you notice how the Hawaiian people spoke and dressed? Draw pictures showing the clothes worn by Hawaiians. What language do they speak? Learn some words to teach the class when you return. What kinds of foods did you eat in Hawaii? Be prepared to tell the class about them.

6. A luau is a Hawaiian feast. Plan a luau for the class. Make a list of the Hawaiian foods that they will eat and the activities that they will enjoy.

From *Kids on the Go* by John Haberberger • ©1994 • Teacher Ideas Press • P.O. Box 6633 • Englewood, CO 80155-6633

IDAHO

Parents, have your child complete
___ questions and ___ activities.

Questions

1. Idaho is a northwestern state. Give the names of the states that border Idaho.

2. What is the capital city of Idaho?

3. The Shoshone Indians called Idaho "ee-da-how." What does this name mean?

4. The state nickname is the Gem State. Why do you think Idaho was given this name? What is the state gem?

5. Idaho is in two time zones. Give the names of the two zones. Explain what happens when you travel from one time zone to another. What must you remember to do to your watch? Explain why there are different time zones across the United States.

6. Idaho is famous for its potatoes, and today the single largest industry in the state is farming. Explain what makes Idaho's farmlands so productive.

7. Tourism is also a large industry in Idaho. Why do you think so many people visit Idaho? Give some examples of things to do and see in the state.

Activities

1. Keep a diary or journal of your travels in Idaho, or make a photo scrapbook of your trip.

2. Hells Canyon, the deepest canyon in North America, is in Idaho. Prepare a report on how the canyon was formed. Tell where it is located, how deep it is, and other interesting facts you learned.

3. Craters of the Moon National Monument is near Arco. Draw a picture or construct a model of the formations. Explain what caused these formations eons ago.

4. Philo T. Farnsworth, of Rigby, invented what we now call television. Imagine that you are an inventor. Create a television of the future, draw a picture of it, and write about the features it has and the things it can do. Be creative.

5. Draw a map of Idaho. Your map should include major cities, Craters of the Moon National Monument, Hells Canyon, and the Snake River.

From *Kids on the Go* by John Haberberger • ©1994 • Teacher Ideas Press • P.O. Box 6633 • Englewood, CO 80155-6633

ILLINOIS

Parents, have your child complete
___ questions and ___ activities.

Questions

1. Name the capital city of Illinois. Where in the state is the city located?

2. On what date did Illinois enter the Union?

3. Name the oldest settlement in the state and give the date that it was settled.

4. Explain why Illinois is called the Land of Lincoln.

5. The state takes its name from the Native Americans who lived in the valley of the Illinois River. What did they call themselves and what did their name mean?

6. Monmouth was the birthplace of Wyatt Earp. Who was Wyatt Earp?

7. The world headquarters of the John Deere Company is in Moline. What did John Deere do in 1837 that was so important to farming?

8. Barbed wire was invented in the city of DeKalb. What is barbed wire? Who is most likely to use barbed wire?

Activities

1. Design a Land of Lincoln T-shirt.

2. At the Lincoln Log Cabin State Historic Site, near Charleston, is the Thomas Lincoln Log Cabin, reconstructed as it was when Abraham Lincoln's father built it in 1837. If you saw this cabin, draw a picture of it. Compare it with your house. Show how they are alike and different, using the Venn diagram. Make a model of a log cabin.

3. Olney is locally famous as the "home of the white squirrels." The town has a population of about 800 of these unusual albino squirrels. Write a short story explaining where these squirrels came from and how they came to live in Olney.

4. If you went to Springfield and saw any of the Lincoln shrines or traveled the Lincoln Heritage Trail, write a letter to a friend telling about the things you saw and learned.

5. Draw a map of Illinois. Your map should include major cities, the Mississippi River, the Illinois River, Lake Michigan, and the Lincoln Log Cabin State Historic Site.

CHICAGO, ILLINOIS

Parents, have your child complete
___ questions and ___ activities.

Questions

1. Illinois is a Great Lakes state. Name the lake that Chicago faces.

2. What did Native Americans call the city of Chicago?

3. Many of Chicago's important areas are found along the city's famous lakefront. If you visited the lakefront, write about the things that you saw and did.

4. The Gold Coast is a well-to-do neighborhood. Why is it called the Gold Coast?

5. The Loop is considered the center of the city. The Marshall Field's department store, in the Loop, is one of the most famous stores in the world. If you went to this store, what did you like best about it?

6. Chicago is home to the Sears Tower and the John Hancock Center, two very tall buildings. Which one is taller? Count the stories. How high are the buildings in feet?

Activities

1. Draw pictures of the Sears Tower and the John Hancock Center. Imagine that you are an architect and design a skyscraper. Draw a picture and build a model of it.

2. Lincoln Park, the largest in Chicago, has a statue of Hans Christian Andersen, who wrote fairy tales. Share a fairy tale with the class when you return. What are some of the elements of a fairy tale? Write your own fairy tale.

3. Lincoln Park also has a zoo that houses a large collection of exotic and endangered species. What does *endangered* mean? Name five endangered animals and draw pictures of them.

4. The Robie House is a fine example of a prairie house. If you saw the Robie House, draw a picture of it. When you return, share with the class what you learned about the house and life on the frontier.

5. The John G. Shedd Aquarium is the world's largest indoor aquarium. If you visited this aquarium, write about what you saw and learned. Draw pictures of the largest and smallest animals that you saw.

INDIANA

Parents, have your child complete
___ questions and ___ activities.

Questions

1. Name the capital city of Indiana.

2. Name the oldest town in the state.

3. Explain why the state calls itself the Crossroads of America.

4. Explain why Indiana is called the Hoosier State and Indianans are called Hoosiers. What is the origin of the word *Hoosier*?

5. Indiana is in two time zones, eastern and central. Explain what happens when you go from one time zone to another. What must you do to your watch? Explain why there are different time zones across the United States.

6. Bedford is the center of Indiana's limestone quarrying, one of the state's important industries. What is limestone and how is it used?

7. Indianapolis is famous for the Indianapolis 500 auto race at the Motor Speedway on Memorial Day weekend. When is Memorial Day observed? If the race is 500 miles long and the oval track is two and one-half miles long, how many laps must the cars travel to cover 500 miles?

Activities

1. Design a Hoosier T-shirt.

2. Pretend that you are racing in the Indy 500. Draw a picture of the car you are driving. If you win the race, what will you do with the prize money?

3. At Wyandotte are the Wyandotte Caves. If you went on a tour of the caves, describe what you saw. How did being in a cave make you feel?

4. Brazil, Indiana, is a mining center where coal is taken from huge open strip mines. What is coal? What are some uses of coal? Explain what open strip mining is. Draw a picture of a mine.

5. At the Lincoln Boyhood National Memorial and Lincoln State Park is the Lincoln Living Historical Farm with a furnished log cabin similar to the one the Lincolns lived in. If you visited this memorial, draw a picture of the log cabin or make a model of it.

6. Keep a diary or journal of your travels in Indiana or make a photo scrapbook of your trip.

IOWA

Parents, have your child complete
___ questions and ___ activities.

Questions

1. What is the capital city of Iowa?

2. Iowa is called the Hawkeye State. Explain why it was given that name.

3. The Sioux Indians had their own name for Iowa. What was their name for the state? Why do you think they chose to call it by that name?

4. Buffalo Bill Cody was born in Iowa. How did he get his nickname? Where is he buried?

5. Name the rivers that are found on the eastern and western boundaries of the state. What is the benefit of having these two navigable rivers nearby?

6. Iowa produces more hogs than any other place in the world. What foods do we get from hogs?

7. The Delicious apple was "born" in Iowa. What is the story of the origin of the Delicious apple?

Activities

1. Design a license plate for Iowa that uses the state nickname, the Hawkeye State, or the Sioux name you found.

2. Iowa is a major producer of soybeans. Prepare a report on soybeans. Explain how they are grown and used. Get some beans and grow them in class when you return.

3. Each summer the *Des Moines Register* sponsors RAGBRAI, which is a week-long bicycle trip across the state. Prepare a report on RAGBRAI. Tell how it got started, how long it has been going on, the route taken across the state, and what the letters in the acronym stand for.

4. Create the perfect bicycle to use on the RAGBRAI ride. You will be on your bike for many hours each day so use your imagination. Make this a dream cycle. Draw a picture of it and explain the different things you have added to it.

5. The National Hot Air Balloon Championship is held in Indianola each year. Design a hot air balloon.

KANSAS

Parents, have your child complete
___ questions and ___ activities.

Questions

1. Kansas is near the center of our country. Name the four states that border Kansas.

2. Name the capital city of Kansas.

3. Name the largest city in Kansas.

4. Kansas is called the Sunflower State and the Jayhawker State. Explain why it has these two nicknames.

5. Kansas records more tornadoes than any other state. What is a tornado? What should you do if you see one? Draw a picture of a tornado.

6. Kansas is known as the "breadbasket of the nation." What does that mean?

7. In the 1800s millions of buffalo roamed the plains around Dodge City, Kansas. By 1875 the buffalo were nearly exterminated. Who killed the buffalo and for what reason?

Activities

1. Design a license plate using either the Sunflower State or the Jayhawker State nickname.

2. The state flower is the sunflower. What are some uses for the sunflower? Draw a picture of a sunflower.

3. Abilene was once famous as a "cow town," and Dodge City was the cowboy capital of the Southwest. Describe what life was like then for the people of the towns.

4. Imagine that you were a cowboy on a cattle drive to Abilene or Dodge City. Describe what life was like for the cowboy. Draw a picture of a cowboy. Would you have wanted to be a cowboy? Write why or why not.

5. Draw a map of Kansas. Your map should include major cities, Abilene, Dodge City, the Dust Bowl region, the Arkansas River, the Chisholm Trail (where it used to be), and the geographical center of the United States.

6. Have you read *The Wizard of Oz*? If you have, then you are familiar with the Gale farm in Kansas. Draw a picture of this farm.

KENTUCKY

Parents, have your child complete
___ questions and ___ activities.

Questions

1. Name the capital city of Kentucky.

2. Kentucky is called the Bluegrass State. Explain why it has this name. What makes the grass look blue?

3. Fort Knox, outside of Louisville, has one of the best security systems in the nation. Why is Fort Knox important? What is kept there?

4. Kentucky is famous for the breeding and training of thoroughbred horses, an industry that is showcased at the Kentucky Horse Park near Lexington. If you visited the park, write about what you saw and did. Write about one new thing you learned about horses.

5. Louisville, called Derby City, is famous for the annual running of the Kentucky Derby. Race horses sometimes have unusual names. What is the name of this year's derby winner? Do you own a horse? If so, what is its name?

6. Mammoth Cave National Park has the world's longest cave. If you took a tour of the cave, list nine things that you saw. What are stalactites and stalagmites?

7. Do you like sports cars? In Bowling Green is the GM Corvette plant and a Corvette museum. Compare a 1964 Corvette with this year's model. Show how they are alike and different, using the Venn diagram. Draw pictures of the two cars.

Activities

1. Design a poster that shows the state motto, United We Stand, Divided We Fall.

2. Design a license plate using the horse theme.

3. The Kentucky Horse Park features the Parade of Breeds Show from April to mid-October. The parade features examples of more than forty breeds of horses. If you saw the parade, write which breed was your favorite. Draw pictures of five breeds and name the breeds.

4. Design a sports car and give some details about it: type and size of engine, type of transmission, top speed, and any special features.

5. Draw a map of Kentucky. Your map should include major cities, the Ohio River, the Cumberland Gap, Mammoth Cave National Park, Fort Knox, and Boonesboro.

From *Kids on the Go* by John Haberberger • ©1994 • Teacher Ideas Press • P.O. Box 6633 • Englewood, CO 80155-6633

LOUISIANA

Parents, have your child complete
___ questions and ___ activities.

Questions

1. Louisiana is in the Deep South. Name the states that border Louisiana.

2. The Mississippi River forms the eastern boundary of the state. Into what body of water does the Mississippi flow?

3. Name the capital city of Louisiana.

4. Louisiana has three nicknames: Bayou State, Sportsman's Paradise, and Pelican State. Explain why it has these names.

5. Plantations are found throughout the state. What is a plantation?

6. Louisiana is a land of bayous. What is a bayou?

7. List five things special to Louisiana that you saw on your visit.

8. Lake Pontchartrain is a brackish lake. What does *brackish* mean?

9. Louisiana is known for its Cajun culture. Who were the original Cajuns? What is the origin of the word Cajun?

Activities

1. Make a map of Louisiana. The map should include major cities, Lake Pontchartrain, and the Mississippi River.

2. Design a license plate using one of the state nicknames: Bayou State, Sportsman's Paradise, or Pelican State.

3. The state bird is the Eastern brown pelican. Draw a picture of the bird.

4. In Baton Rouge is the Myrtles Plantation, which is known as one of "America's most haunted mansions." Read about this famous mansion. Either draw a picture or build a model of your own haunted mansion. Write a history of your mansion telling how it became haunted. You could also write a short story about the mansion and the "ghosts" that occupy it.

5. Keep a diary or journal of your travels in Louisiana or make a photo scrapbook of your visit.

6. Make a travel brochure for the state of Louisiana.

7. Cajun food is a cuisine popular in Louisiana. What gives Cajun food its special, unique flavor? Prepare a dinner menu using Cajun food.

From *Kids on the Go* by John Haberberger • ©1994 • Teacher Ideas Press • P.O. Box 6633 • Englewood, CO 80155-6633

NEW ORLEANS, LOUISIANA

Parents, have your child complete
___ questions and ___ activities.

Questions

1. For whom is New Orleans named?

2. Where in Louisiana is New Orleans located? On what major river is the city situated?

3. The population of New Orleans includes Creoles and Cajuns. Who are the Creoles? Who are the Cajuns?

4. Mardi Gras is a famous celebration that occurs yearly in New Orleans. What do the words *Mardi Gras* mean? At what time of the year does Mardi Gras take place?

5. New Orleans is famous for its Creole cuisine. If you had any Creole food, how did it taste? What did you have? Did you enjoy it? Write why or why not.

6. The Lake Pontchartrain Causeway is the world's longest overwater bridge. How long is the bridge?

7. The Louisiana Superdome is an unusual-looking building. What does it look like to you? What is the Superdome used for?

8. Among tourists, New Orleans is famous for its Vieux Carré, or French Quarter. If you visited this area of the city, write about the things you saw.

Activities

1. Talk with some museum guides about the Creole and Cajun cultures. Or if possible, try to meet some people of Creole or Cajun heritage. Find out about their ancestors. Using the Venn diagram, show how these groups are alike and different.

2. Mardi Gras activities include torchlight parades, street dancing, costume balls, and masquerades. Design a costume for a Mardi Gras ball. Draw a picture of it or, when you get home, make the costume to show the class.

3. The French Quarter Festival is in mid-April. If you attended the festival, write about what you saw and did.

4. In New Orleans you will see paddle-wheel and stern-wheel steamboats on the Mississippi River. Draw a picture of each type of boat and compare the two. Show how they are alike and different, using the Venn diagram.

5. If you took a tour of the Louisiana bayous draw a picture of the bayou. What is a bayou? What animals live in the bayous? What kind of trees did you see?

From *Kids on the Go* by John Haberberger • ©1994 • Teacher Ideas Press • P.O. Box 6633 • Englewood, CO 80155-6633

MAINE

Parents, have your child complete
___ questions and ___ activities.

Questions

1. Name the capital city of Maine.

2. Name the largest city in the state.

3. Explain why Maine is called the Pine Tree State.

4. Maine is famous for its lobsters. How are lobsters caught and cooked?

5. Name the five islands in the group called the Cranberry Isles.

6. If you visited Acadia National Park, you may have seen and heard Thunder Hole. Explain why it has this name.

7. The nation's northeasternmost city is in Maine. What is the name of that city?

8. Bath Iron Works, in Bath, has been building ships since 1889. If you visited the shipyards, describe what you saw. Did you get to see the launching of a ship? If so, write about it.

9. Maine has the highest tides in the country. Explain what a tide is. What causes this phenomenon?

Activities

1. Create a new dish that uses lobster. Write the recipe.

2. When you return from your trip, share a cranberry product with the class.

3. If you visited the shipyards at Bath, draw pictures of some of the different ships you saw. Label each ship.

4. Moosehead Lake is located in the heart of Maine's North Woods. Here is found the largest moose population in the continental United States. Draw pictures of a moose and a deer. Compare the two animals. Show how they are alike and different, using the Venn diagram.

5. Draw a map of Maine. Your map should include major cities, Moosehead Lake, Acadia National Park, the lighthouse Portland Head Light, Mount Katahdin, and the Atlantic Ocean.

6. Make a travel brochure for the state of Maine.

From *Kids on the Go* by John Haberberger • ©1994 • Teacher Ideas Press • P.O. Box 6633 • Englewood, CO 80155-6633

MARYLAND

Parents, have your child complete
___ questions and ___ activities.

Questions

1. Maryland takes its name from the wife of Charles I, King of England. What was her name?

2. Maryland was one of the original thirteen colonies and was the seventh state to enter the Union. Give the date when Maryland entered the Union. Name the original thirteen colonies.

3. In 1694 Annapolis became the capital of Maryland. What city was the first capital of Maryland?

4. Maryland is called the Old Line State and the Free State. Explain the meanings of these two nicknames.

5. The U.S. Naval Academy, in Annapolis, is where men and women train to be officers in the navy. Would you want to serve our country in the navy? Write why or why not.

6. In October 1814 the British attacked the city of Baltimore but gave up when they couldn't take Fort McHenry. It was then that Francis Scott Key wrote the "Star-Spangled Banner," our national anthem. What is an anthem? What inspired Key to write the words he did?

Activities

1. Draw a map showing the original thirteen colonies.

2. Design a license plate using one of the state nicknames, Old Line State or Free State.

3. Draw a picture of yourself in a navy uniform.

4. Compose a new national anthem for our country. Your composition can be words, music, or both words and music. Do you prefer your anthem or the "Star-Spangled Banner"? Share your anthem with the class and take a survey to find out which anthem your classmates prefer.

5. Because Maryland is on the Chesapeake Bay and the Atlantic Ocean, fresh seafood is readily available. If you eat at a restaurant, try a fish entree that is new for you. If you tried a new dish, write the name of it and tell if you liked it or not.

6. List five water sports that you could do at the bay or ocean. Draw yourself doing one of these sports.

7. Draw a map of Maryland. Your map should include the Atlantic Ocean, Chesapeake Bay, the Potomac River, Baltimore, and Washington, D.C.

From *Kids on the Go* by John Haberberger • ©1994 • Teacher Ideas Press • P.O. Box 6633 • Englewood, CO 80155-6633

MASSACHUSETTS

Parents, have your child complete
___ questions and ___ activities.

Questions

1. Name the capital city of Massachusetts.

2. Massachusetts was the sixth of the original states. On what date did Massachusetts enter the Union? How many years has Massachusetts been a state?

3. Cape Cod is said to face "four seas." Name the four bodies of water Cape Cod faces.

4. Cape Cod has an unusual shape. What does it look like to you?

5. Massachusetts is an Indian name given to the area. What does the name mean?

6. Concord shares with Lexington the title of Birthplace of the Republic. Explain why the town was named Concord.

7. The first organized fight of the War of Independence was in Lexington on April 19, 1775. Explain what happened during the Battle of Lexington.

8. Salem is known for the infamous witch trials of 1692. If you visited Salem, write what you learned about the witch hunt.

Activities

1. Draw a map of Massachusetts. Your map should include major cities, Cape Cod and the "four seas" it faces, Salem, Martha's Vineyard, Nantucket, Concord, Lexington, and Cambridge.

2. The famous Concord grape was developed in Concord in 1849. Draw a picture of a bunch of Concord grapes. Do these grapes have seeds or are they seedless? What color are they?

3. If you read about the Battle of Lexington, draw a picture showing the battle. Draw the British soldiers and Minutemen as they were dressed then. Why were they called Minutemen?

4. Make a travel brochure for the state of Massachusetts.

5. James Naismith invented the game of basketball at a Springfield YMCA, using two peach baskets and a soccer ball. Imagine that you work for an elementary school and are asked to come up with a new indoor game. Write about your idea for a game. Explain how to play it and give the rules. What equipment is needed?

BOSTON, MASSACHUSETTS

Parents, have your child complete
___ questions and ___ activities.

Questions

1. Greater Boston consists of eighty-three cities and towns. Did you visit any of them? List ten of the cities and towns in alphabetical order.

2. Boston is a great place for walkers, and walking tours are popular with visitors. It you went walking or took a walking tour, write about the things that you saw and did.

3. Paul Revere is famous in America's history. Who was Paul Revere and why was his ride important? What was the importance of Old North Church?

4. The American Revolution began in Boston in 1770 shortly after what has been called the Boston Massacre. Explain what happened in this massacre.

5. The Boston Tea Party Ship and Museum is found in Boston. What was the Boston Tea Party?

6. The Boston Marathon is held every year on the third Monday in April. What is a marathon? How many miles long is it?

Activities

1. If you saw Paul Revere's house and Old North Church, draw pictures of them. Old North Church is the oldest church building in Boston. Compare it with the church that you attend or a church building that you know in your home city. Using the Venn diagram, show how they are alike and different.

2. Draw a picture of the Boston Tea Party ship.

3. Design a Boston Marathon T-shirt.

4. Because Boston is next to the Atlantic Ocean, fresh seafood is plentiful. Did you eat a new seafood dish? What was it called? Did you like it? Be creative and invent a dish using lobster or crab. List the ingredients and write the recipe.

5. Plan a walking tour of your home city or your neighborhood. Tell where the tour begins and ends. List the places of interest that the visitor will see.

From *Kids on the Go* by John Haberberger • ©1994 • Teacher Ideas Press • P.O. Box 6633 • Englewood, CO 80155-6633

MICHIGAN

Parents, have your child complete
___ questions and ___ activities.

Questions

1. Name the capital city of Michigan.

2. The two Michigan peninsulas are touched by four of the Great Lakes. Name the four lakes. What is a peninsula?

3. Michigan is called the Wolverine State. What is a wolverine?

4. Explain the origin of the name of the town Ann Arbor.

5. Battle Creek was made famous by two cereal giants, W. K. Kellogg and C. W. Post. Name the grains from which cereal is made. Name five Kellogg cereals and five Post cereals. What is your favorite cereal?

6. Detroit is the city that put the world on wheels. Detroit was the birthplace of the assembly line and mass production in the automobile industry. What is an assembly line?

7. Kalamazoo is an unusual name. What does the name mean?

8. Sault Ste. Marie is known for the famous locks of the St. Marys River. Explain the meaning of the name Sault Ste. Marie. How is it pronounced?

Activities

1. Design a wolverine T-shirt.

2. Draw a map of Michigan. Your map should include major cities, the four Great Lakes touching Michigan, the bridge connecting the two peninsulas, the locks at Sault Ste. Marie, and the United States/Canada boundary line.

3. Imagine that you work for the Kellogg or Post company and you are asked to create a new cold cereal. Describe your new cereal and draw a picture of the cereal box.

4. Think of something your class could make using an assembly line and develop a plan for doing it. When you return, the class can look at your plan with you and become involved in your idea.

5. Make a travel brochure for the state of Michigan.

6. Imagine that you work for the Ford Motor Company and you are asked to design a car for the future. Draw a picture or make a model of your car.

From *Kids on the Go* by John Haberberger • ©1994 • Teacher Ideas Press • P.O. Box 6633 • Englewood, CO 80155-6633

MINNESOTA

Parents, have your child complete
___ questions and ___ activities.

Questions

1. Name the four states and the two Canadian provinces that border Minnesota. Name the Great Lake that touches Minnesota.

2. Name the capital city of Minnesota.

3. Minnesota is called the Gopher State and the North Star State. What are the meanings of these two names?

4. Although Minnesota borders on Canada and is 1,000 miles from either ocean, it is considered a seaboard state. Explain why Minnesota is considered a seaboard state.

5. Minnesota is called the land of 10,000 lakes. Legend says that the lakes were stamped out by the hooves of Paul Bunyan's giant blue ox, Babe. Who was Paul Bunyan? Write how you think the lakes were formed.

6. Name the major river that begins in Minnesota and flows the length of the United States. Name the lake that is the source of this river.

Activities

1. Design a license plate using either the Gopher State or North Star State nickname.

2. Draw a map of Minnesota. Your map should include major cities, the Mississippi River, Lake Superior, Lake Itasca, and International Falls.

3. Minnesota has many thousands of lakes. If you drew a map for activity 2, now draw ten lakes that you want to add to Minnesota. Print the names of your ten lakes and write why you chose the names.

4. The story of Paul Bunyan is a tall tale. Read a Paul Bunyan story to the class when you return, write your own Paul Bunyan story, or create your own tall tale character and write a story.

5. Minnesota has spectacular wilderness areas. Plan a vacation for your family in the Boundary Waters Canoe Area. You will be traveling by canoe and camping. The vacation will last one week. List the food and supplies that you will need. Draw a map of the area and indicate the places where you will camp each night. Write what you will do during the days of this vacation.

From *Kids on the Go* by John Haberberger • ©1994 • Teacher Ideas Press • P.O. Box 6633 • Englewood, CO 80155-6633

MINNEAPOLIS/ST. PAUL, MINNESOTA

Parents, have your child complete
___ questions and ___ activities.

Questions

1. The word Minneapolis comes from a Sioux word and a Greek word. What are the two words and what do they mean?

2. St. Paul began as a settlement known as Pig's Eye. Explain the origin of this name. How did the city come to be called St. Paul?

3. Name the major river that flows between the two cities. Where does this river begin?

4. In Minneapolis is St. Anthony Falls. What was the importance of the community of St. Anthony that developed there?

5. St. Paul is the state capital of Minnesota. The state capitol building has one of the largest self-supporting marble domes in the world. Twenty-one varieties of marble were used in its construction. If you are able to visit the capitol, draw a picture of this marble dome and write what you learned about its construction.

6. You may see an authentic Mississippi River stern-wheeler. If you did, compare a stern-wheeler to a boat of today. Show how they are alike and different, using the Venn diagram.

Activities

1. The riverboat can take you on a cruise to historic Fort Snelling near where the city of St. Paul began. If you went there, describe what you saw.

2. Minnesota is called the land of 10,000 lakes. Natives of the state say that the lakes were stamped out by the hooves of Paul Bunyan's giant blue ox, Babe. Paul Bunyan stories are tall tales. Here are some ideas for Paul: (1) draw pictures or make models of Paul and Babe, (2) choose a Paul Bunyan story to read to the class, (3) write about the origin of Paul Bunyan, or (4) write your own Paul Bunyan story.

3. Design a Pig's Eye T-shirt for St. Paul residents.

4. Draw a map of the Twin Cities. Your map should include the Mississippi River, the Minnesota River, St. Anthony Falls, Fort Snelling, and the international airport.

5. What is marble? Imagine that you are a sculptor and design a marble sculpture for your front yard.

From *Kids on the Go* by John Haberberger • ©1994 • Teacher Ideas Press • P.O. Box 6633 • Englewood, CO 80155-6633

MISSISSIPPI

Parents, have your child complete
___ questions and ___ activities.

Questions

1. Name the capital city of Mississippi.

2. Mississippi is called the Magnolia State. Who selected the magnolia as the state flower in 1900?

3. The word *Mississippi* comes from the Choctaw Indian language. What does Mississippi mean?

4. For centuries the area that is now Mississippi was home to which three large Indian nations?

5. Mississippi shows the past in the many historic antebellum mansions found there. What does *antebellum* mean? If you visited a mansion, describe what you saw. Draw pictures of the mansion and your own home.

6. The John C. Stennis Space Center near Picayune is where the space shuttle main engines are tested. If you visited the space center, write about what you saw and did. Write about one new thing you learned. Why is the space shuttle important? What would you choose to send into space in the shuttle? Why is space exploration important?

7. Name the four islands found at the Gulf Islands National Seashore. Explain why Ship island is split in two.

Activities

1. Draw a picture of a magnolia.

2. Mississippi is the largest manufacturer of upholstered furniture. Design some furniture of the future.

3. The Natchez Trace was the most heavily traveled road in the lower Mississippi Valley in the early 1800s. What is a trace? Draw a map of Mississippi that shows the Natchez Trace, from start to finish.

4. The Mississippi Petrified Forest, in Flora, has giant trees that are 36 million years old. If you visited the forest, describe what you saw. Explain the process or stages a tree goes through to become petrified.

5. The Shrimp Festival is celebrated at Biloxi, on the waters of the Gulf of Mexico, the first weekend in June. The boats are decorated and the Blessing of the Fleet takes place. Why do you think the boats are blessed? Draw a picture of a shrimp boat that is decorated, or design your own decorations for shrimp boat.

From Kids on the Go by John Haberberger • ©1994 • Teacher Ideas Press • P.O. Box 6633 • Englewood, CO 80155-6633

MISSOURI

Parents, have your child complete
___ questions and ___ activities.

Questions

1. Missouri has many neighbors. Name the eight states that border Missouri.

2. What major river forms the eastern boundary of Missouri?

3. Name the capital city of Missouri.

4. Explain why Missouri is called the Show Me State.

5. The Pony Express began in St. Joseph, Missouri. What was the Pony Express? Who performs that service today? Would you like to have been a rider? Why or why not?

6. Hannibal is famous as the hometown of the writer Mark Twain. What was his real name? Name two books that he wrote.

7. Missouri was the site of many of Daniel Boone's legendary adventures. Who was Daniel Boone?

8. Lake of the Ozarks has a very irregular 1,372-mile shoreline. Pretend that you are flying over the lake. When you look down, what does the lake look like to you? List five water activities you could do at the lake.

Activities

1. Design a license plate using the Show Me State nickname.

2. The Hallmark greeting card company was started by a Missourian. Design a greeting card to send to a friend, a Mother's Day or Father's Day card, or a birthday card.

3. Read *The Adventures of Tom Sawyer* or *The Adventures of Huckleberry Finn*. Share the stories with the class when you return.

4. If you read the Tom Sawyer or Huck Finn stories, try your hand at writing a short story about them to share with the class.

5. Some notorious outlaws from the frontier days called Missouri home. Draw a wanted poster for one of these outlaws.

6. Draw a map of Missouri. Your map should include major cities, the Mississippi River, the Missouri River, Hannibal, Mark Twain National Forest, the Lake of the Ozarks, and the Ozark Mountains.

ST. LOUIS, MISSOURI

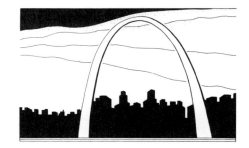

Parents, have your child complete
___ questions and ___ activities.

Questions

1. St. Louis is one of the oldest settlements in the Mississippi Valley. For whom was the city named?

2. Write the names of the two rivers that meet near St. Louis. Explain why these rivers are important.

3. In what part of the state is the city located?

4. The Gateway Arch is located in St. Louis. Write a short paragraph that tells what the arch symbolizes. How high is the arch?

5. At the zoo in Forest Park is the Living World Education Center. If you visited the center, write a letter to the class telling them what you saw there.

6. In the St. Louis Cathedral is the largest collection of mosaic art in the world. What is mosaic art?

7. Near St. Louis is Purina Farms where you can find domestic animals, petting areas, animal demonstrations, and other things. What is a domestic animal? Make a list of five domestic animals.

8. The Magic House is in the St. Louis Children's Museum. If you went there, write about what you saw and did.

Activities

1. Draw a picture of the Gateway Arch.

2. If you saw the mosaic art at the cathedral, either draw a picture of a mosaic section or make one that you saw.

3. Draw a picture of something to put in the Magic House.

4. The nearby river town of Washington is known as the corncob pipe capital of the world. What is a corncob pipe? Draw a picture of one.

5. Using the Venn diagram, compare two domestic animals. Show how they are alike and different.

6. Riverboat cruises are available for visitors. If you took a cruise or saw a riverboat, draw a picture of it.

7. If you visited the Museum of Westward Expansion at the Gateway Arch, you saw exhibits showing people and events of nineteenth-century western America. How did people dress in those days? Use the Venn diagram to compare boys' or girls' clothing of then and now. Draw a picture of a boy or girl dressed in the clothes of that era.

From *Kids on the Go* by John Haberberger • ©1994 • Teacher Ideas Press • P.O. Box 6633 • Englewood, CO 80155-6633

MONTANA

Parents, have your child complete
___ questions and ___ activities.

Questions

1. Montana is a western state. Give the names of the states that border Montana.

2. Explain how Montana got its name.

3. What is the capital city of Montana?

4. Explain why Montana is called the Treasure State and Big Sky Country.

5. Why is Hell Creek of interest to people who study dinosaurs?

6. The Missouri River begins in Montana. Look at a map of Montana and find the Missouri. What is unusual about the way it flows?

7. In Glacier National Park you will find more than fifty glaciers. What is a glacier? When a glacier moves what does it do to the land?

8. Custer's Last Stand took place in Montana in 1876. What Native Americans did Custer's troops fight? What river was the site of the battle?

Activities

1. There are 25 major dams on the rivers of Montana. Build a model of one or draw a picture of one. Give some facts about the dam. Explain how it was built. What is hydroelectric power?

2. Mining is an important industry in Montana. Virginia City is probably the most famous mining town. Prepare a report about the history of Virginia City.

3. Give a demonstration of how to pan for gold. Explain the equipment and how it is used.

4. You are an artist at the famous battle between Custer and the Sioux and Cheyenne Nations. Draw a picture of the battle showing how Custer's soldiers and their opponents looked in battle.

5. Draw a map of Montana. Your map should include major cities, the Missouri River, the Yellowstone River, Little Bighorn Battlefield National Monument, Glacier National Park, and the Rocky Mountains.

NEBRASKA

Parents, have your child complete
___ questions and ___ activities.

Questions

1. What is the capital city of Nebraska?

2. Nebraska is called the Cornhusker State. Explain why it was given this name.

3. Nebraska is primarily prairie land. What is a prairie?

4. Nebraska is bordered by six states. Give the names of those states.

5. The southern boundary line with Kansas is perfectly straight. Legend credits this to Febold Feboldson, the Paul Bunyan of the Great Plains. Explain the legend of the straight boundary line.

6. Farming is big business in Nebraska. The state is a leading producer of many grains. List five of these grains.

7. The Homestead National Monument is found near Beatrice. What is significant about this site? Explain why it is a national monument. If you visited the monument, list the other historical items on display. Draw a picture of the cabin on the land. What was the Homestead Act of 1862?

Activities

1. Design a state license plate using Cornhusker State, the Nebraska state nickname.

2. Pretend that you are living in the 1880s. Under the conditions of the Homestead Act you are given 160 acres of land to live on and work for five years. Draw a map of your 160 acres. On the map show your cabin and barn, your fields, and whatever else you choose to have. List what crops you will grow and your plans for the future. You could also build a model of your cabin. Brainstorm a list of possible problems you might encounter living on the plains during that time.

3. Chimney Rock is found near Bayard. Why was this rock important to the early pioneers? If you saw the rock, draw a picture of it.

4. Arbor Day was started in Nebraska. What is the meaning of Arbor Day? Why is it important? Plant a tree in your backyard or at your school.

5. Imagine that you are an early pioneer traveling across the Nebraska prairie in a covered wagon. Make a list of the supplies that you think you will need on your journey. Draw a picture of the covered wagon or make a model of it.

From *Kids on the Go* by John Haberberger • ©1994 • Teacher Ideas Press • P.O. Box 6633 • Englewood, CO 80155-6633

NEVADA

Parents, have your child complete
___ questions and ___ activities.

Questions

1. Nevada is a western state. Name the states that border Nevada.

2. Name the capital city of Nevada.

3. What is the largest city in the state?

4. Nevada is called the Silver State. Explain why it has this nickname.

5. At Great Basin National Park you will find ecologic and geologic attractions. If you visited the park, write about the things you saw there. If you went in the caves, describe what you saw. Draw a picture of the inside of the caves. Explain how the caves were formed.

6. How did Las Vegas get started? Write a short history of this famous city.

7. Hoover Dam, a giant concrete structure, is found south of Las Vegas. The dam was built on which river? If you saw the dam, draw a picture of it.

Activities

1. Draw a picture of the Lexington arch found at Great Basin National Park. Explain how it was formed.

2. Turquoise is found in Nevada. What color is turquoise? Design a piece of jewelry using turquoise.

3. Draw a picture of a desert. Your picture should include different plants and animals found there. Label the plants and animals in your picture.

4. If you visited a casino, draw a picture of it, outside and inside. Write about any special attractions that you saw at the casino.

5. Draw a map of Nevada. Your map should include major cities, Hoover Dam, Great Basin National Park, and Lake Tahoe.

NEW HAMPSHIRE

Parents, have your child complete
___ questions and ___ activities.

Questions

1. Name the capital city of New Hampshire.

2. Name the states that border New Hampshire.

3. The elevation of New Hampshire ranges from sea level to 6,288 feet. What is the highest point in the state?

4. New Hampshire is a year-round vacation state, offering a variety of recreational opportunities within its six regions. Name the six regions of the state.

5. Explain why New Hampshire is called the Granite State. What is granite?

6. Timberline in the Rocky Mountains is near 10,000 feet, but timberline on Mount Washington is about 4,000 feet. What is timberline? Explain why it is at such a low elevation on Mount Washington.

7. When crossing the Continental Divide in the Rocky Mountains you travel over a pass, but in New Hampshire these passes go by another name. They are called "notches." Why do you think the gaps in the New Hampshire mountains are called notches?

Activities

1. Draw a map of New Hampshire. Your map should include major cities, the six regions of the state, Mount Washington, Lake Winnipesaukee, and the Appalachian Trail.

2. Draw a picture of Mount Washington. Your picture should include the timberline, the cog railway, and the road to the top.

3. Plan a family vacation in New Hampshire. Make a vacation schedule for two weeks. Plan and write about where you will go, what you will do, and how long you will stay at each place. Your vacation could be a backpacking trip on the Appalachian Trail.

4. At Franconia Notch State Park is the Old Man of the Mountains, a craggy likeness of a man's face that is forty feet high. It is also known as the "Great Stone Face." If you were at the park and saw this face, draw a picture of it. What do you think caused this figure to appear in the stone?

5. Design a Granite State T-shirt.

From *Kids on the Go* by John Haberberger • ©1994 • Teacher Ideas Press • P.O. Box 6633 • Englewood, CO 80155-6633

NEW JERSEY

Parents, have your child complete
___ questions and ___ activities.

Questions

1. Name the capital city of New Jersey.

2. Name the largest city in the state.

3. New Jersey was the third of the original thirteen states to enter the Union. On what date did New Jersey enter the Union?

4. The Meadowlands, a sports complex, hosts two NFL football teams: the New York Giants and the New York Jets. Explain why these two New York teams play in New Jersey.

5. With its many lakes, ponds, rivers, and streams, New Jersey is a popular place for anglers. What is an angler?

6. What popular board game is based on Atlantic City?

7. New Jersey is called the Garden State. If you were planning a garden, what would you plant? Would it be a vegetable garden or one with flowers? List the things that you would plant in your garden.

8. Thomas Edison built his laboratory in West Orange, where he worked on many of his inventions. Name three things that Edison invented.

Activities

1. Asbury Park is the birthplace of saltwater taffy. Create a new and unusual taffy flavor and write the recipe for it.

2. Create a board game based on your home city. It might help to "piggyback" on other board games you are familiar with.

3. Are you a football fan? What is your favorite team? Design a new uniform for that team.

4. Draw a picture of the garden you might want to plant. Remember to color your picture.

5. New Jersey is on the Atlantic Ocean and fresh seafood is readily available. If you eat at a restaurant, try a fish entrée that is new for you. Write the name of the new dish and tell if you liked it or not.

6. Draw a map of New Jersey. Your map should include major cities, Atlantic City, West Orange, Asbury Park, the Delaware Bay, and the Atlantic Ocean.

From *Kids on the Go* by John Haberberger • ©1994 • Teacher Ideas Press • P.O. Box 6633 • Englewood, CO 80155-6633

NEW MEXICO

Parents, have your child complete
___ questions and ___ activities.

Questions

1. New Mexico is a southwestern state. Name the states that border New Mexico.

2. Name the capital city of New Mexico.

3. New Mexico is called the Land of Enchantment. Explain why it has this nickname.

4. Native Americans lived in New Mexico for centuries before the arrival of Europeans. Name the peoples who lived there. Explain how the Pueblo Indians got their name. Native Americans were forced to live on reservations as pioneers moved West. What is a reservation? Do you think it was right to treat the Native American people this way? Explain why or why not.

5. Wheeler Peak is the highest point in the state. How high is the peak? Where is it located?

6. Carlsbad Caverns National Park is in New Mexico. There you will see one of the largest caverns in the world, the Carlsbad Cavern, and more than seventy caves. Who was the cowboy who first explored the caverns? Explain how Carlsbad Cavern was formed. How deep is the cavern below the surface? If you took a tour of the cavern, describe what you saw. Draw a picture of it. What are stalactites and stalagmites?

Activities

1. Design a license plate using the Land of Enchantment nickname.

2. Prepare a report on the Native Americans now living in New Mexico. Your report should include their history and how they currently live. If you visited one of the Pueblo groups, tell about what you saw. If you saw a religious ceremony or a special dance, describe it. Take photographs, but only with permission, to share with the class when you return.

3. In September there is a 100-mile bicycle ride around Wheeler Peak. Imagine that you are going to ride in it. Design a dream bicycle to use on this ride. You will be on your bike for many hours, so be creative.

4. New Mexico's state gem is the mineral turquoise. What color is turquoise? Design a piece of jewelry using turquoise.

5. Draw a map of New Mexico. Your map should include major cities, Taos, Wheeler Peak, Carlsbad Caverns, and the Rio Grande River.

6. The world's largest hot air balloon rally is held in Albuquerque each year in October. Imagine that you are entering the rally and design a balloon.

7. Prepare a report on the Hispanic heritage and population of the state of New Mexico. Explain who the Hispanics are and their origin.

From *Kids on the Go* by John Haberberger • ©1994 • Teacher Ideas Press • P.O. Box 6633 • Englewood, CO 80155-6633

NEW YORK

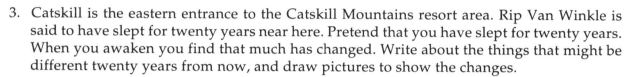

Parents, have your child complete
___ questions and ___ activities.

Questions

1. Name the capital city of New York.

2. Explain why New York is called the Empire State.

3. Catskill is the eastern entrance to the Catskill Mountains resort area. Rip Van Winkle is said to have slept for twenty years near here. Pretend that you have slept for twenty years. When you awaken you find that much has changed. Write about the things that might be different twenty years from now, and draw pictures to show the changes.

4. The Finger Lakes are a popular recreation area in New York. Explain how the lakes were formed. There are eleven lakes. Write their names in alphabetical order. Which lake is the deepest? Which lake is the longest?

5. Lake Placid was the site of the 1980 Winter Olympics. Name five events in the Winter Olympics.

6. Niagara Falls is a popular tourist attraction. The falls are on the borderline with what country? The American Falls is how high? The Canadian Horseshoe is how high? The American Falls is how much higher than the Canadian Horseshoe?

Activities

1. Draw a map of New York. Your map should include major cities, the Finger Lakes, the Hudson River, the Adirondack Park, the Catskill Park, and Niagara Falls.

2. Either write your own Rip Van Winkle story or find the story in a book and share it with the class.

3. Pretend that the Finger Lakes have just recently formed and your job is to name them. Draw the lakes and write the names you choose for each lake.

4. Draw pictures to symbolize five Winter Olympic events.

5. You have volunteered to go over Niagara Falls in a barrel. Design a barrel that will keep you safe from injury. Draw a picture of your barrel and label the different things that you put in it.

6. Make a travel brochure for the state of New York.

From *Kids on the Go* by John Haberberger • ©1994 • Teacher Ideas Press • P.O. Box 6633 • Englewood, CO 80155-6633

NEW YORK CITY, NEW YORK

Parents, have your child complete
___ questions and ___ activities.

Questions

1. New York City was originally called New Amsterdam, but in 1664 the town was renamed New York. The name was changed in honor of what man?

2. Explain why New York City is called the Big Apple.

3. Name the five boroughs of New York City.

4. New York is the nation's most populous city. How many people live in New York City?

5. The Statue of Liberty National Monument is on Liberty Island in Manhattan. What country gave the statue to America? How high is the statue? Why is the statue important?

6. Ellis Island is the most famous port of immigration in the country. Who are immigrants? Is Ellis Island still used as a port of immigration? What is found there now?

7. Central Park was the first formally planned park in the country. If you visited the park, write about what you saw. Is it like any park in your home city?

8. The Empire State Building is the skyscraper that became famous when King Kong climbed it in the movie. How high is the building?

Activities

1. The Bronx Zoo is one of the largest zoos in the world and has many special attractions. If you visited the zoo, write about what you saw and learned. Take photographs to share with classmates when you return.

2. Coney Island is probably the best-known amusement park in the country. If you went there, what was your favorite ride? Be creative and invent a new ride for the park. Describe your ride and explain how it works. Draw a picture of your ride.

3. If you rode on the famous Staten Island ferry, write about the trip. Where did the ferry take you? Draw a picture of the ferryboat. How much did it cost for your family to ride the boat?

4. Design either a Big Apple T-shirt or a T-shirt that shows something about your visit to New York.

5. The New York City Marathon, held in late October, is a famous race. Describe the course of that marathon. How long is a marathon? Design a poster that advertises the marathon.

From *Kids on the Go* by John Haberberger • ©1994 • Teacher Ideas Press • P.O. Box 6633 • Englewood, CO 80155-6633

NORTH CAROLINA

Parents, have your child complete
___ questions and ___ activities.

Questions

1. Name the capital city of North Carolina.

2. Name the largest city in the state.

3. Explain why Cape Hatteras is called the Graveyard of the Atlantic.

4. North Carolina was the twelfth of the original thirteen states to enter the Union. On what date did North Carolina enter the Union?

5. The Fort Raleigh National Historic Site is where the first English colony in America was attempted on Roanoke Island in 1585. The attempt was unsuccessful and the colony disappeared leaving only the crudely scratched word CROATOAN cut into a tree. The colony's disappearance is still a mystery. What are some possible explanations for the disappearance of the colony?

6. North Carolina is called the Tar Heel State, and citizens take pride in being called Tar Heels, a term that dates back to the Civil War. Write a paragraph that explains the Tar Heels story.

7. Kill Devil Hills, near Kitty Hawk, is where the Wright Brothers did their early flying experiments. Give the names of the Wright Brothers. What was the date of their first flight?

Activities

1. Design a license plate using one of the state nicknames, Tar Heel State or Old North State.

2. Draw a map of North Carolina. Your map should include major cities, Roanoke Island, Kitty Hawk, Great Smoky Mountains National Park with the Appalachian Trail, and Cape Hatteras.

3. Draw pictures of the first plane that the Wright Brothers flew and a present-day aircraft. Show how they are alike and different using the Venn diagram. Would you like to be a pilot? Write why or why not.

4. Make a travel brochure for the state of North Carolina.

5. Keep a diary or journal of your travels or make a photo scrapbook of your trip.

From *Kids on the Go* by John Haberberger • ©1994 • Teacher Ideas Press • P.O. Box 6633 • Englewood, CO 80155-6633

NORTH DAKOTA

Parents, have your child complete
___ questions and ___ activities.

Questions

1. North Dakota is at the center of the continent. Give the names of North Dakota's neighboring states.

2. What city in North Dakota is the geographic center of North America?

3. Name the capital city of North Dakota.

4. North Dakota is in two time zones. What are the two zones? Explain what happens when you travel from one time zone to another. What must you remember to do to your watch? Why are there different time zones across the United States?

5. North Dakota has three nicknames: Flickertail State, Sioux State, and Peace Garden State. Choose one of these nicknames and explain why the state was given that name.

6. The Missouri River flows through North Dakota. Where does it begin? Explain why it is called the Big Muddy.

7. North Dakota's wealth is in its soil. List some crops that are grown there. Explain why huge ranches are found in North Dakota.

8. The International Peace Garden is found near Bottineau. What does the park symbolize? If you visited the park, write about what you saw.

Activities

1. Draw a map of North Dakota. Your map should include major cities, the International Peace Garden, the Theodore Roosevelt National Park, Rugby, and Lake Sakakawea (or Sakajawea).

2. Prepare a report on the Theodore Roosevelt National Park. Explain who Roosevelt was and why it is a monument to him. The report should mention the three units of the park and what can be found in each.

3. If you go to the International Peace Garden, take photos or a video and prepare a presentation to share when you return.

4. Design a North Dakota T-shirt that uses one of the state nicknames: Flickertail State, Sioux State, or Peace Garden State.

5. Make a travel brochure for the state of North Dakota.

6. Keep a diary or journal of your travels or make a photo scrapbook of your trip.

From *Kids on the Go* by John Haberberger • ©1994 • Teacher Ideas Press • P.O. Box 6633 • Englewood, CO 80155-6633

OHIO

Parents, have your child complete
___ questions and ___ activities.

Questions

1. Name the capital city of Ohio.

2. The name *Ohio* is taken from an Iroquois Indian word. What is the meaning of the word?

3. Explain why Ohio is called the Buckeye State.

4. Explain why the scarlet carnation was made the state flower.

5. Thomas Edison was from Ohio. Name something that he invented.

6. Akron, best known for its rubber factories, is the "rubber capital of the world." List five things made of rubber.

7. In Chillicothe is the Mound City Group National Monument, which is the burial grounds of a prehistoric Indian culture. Name the Indians who built these mounds.

8. Johnny Appleseed planted some of his orchards in Coshocton. Who was Johnny Appleseed? What is an orchard?

9. Astronauts John Glenn and Neil Armstrong are from Ohio. Would you want to be an astronaut? Write why or why not. Do you think that space exploration is important? Write why or why not.

Activities

1. Wooster claims to have had the first Christmas tree in America. Share the Wooster story with the class. Draw a picture of how you think that tree looked.

2. To celebrate Johnny Appleseed, make something using apples to share with the class, or create a new apple recipe. List the ingredients and write the directions for making it.

3. Both Toledo and Cambridge have glass-making factories. If you visited either city and toured a factory, prepare a report on the glass-making process.

4. If you visited Akron and toured a rubber factory, explain how rubber is made. You could draw pictures to show the steps in the process.

5. Draw a map of Ohio. Your map should include major cities, Lake Erie, Point Pleasant, the Ohio River, Independence Dam State Park, and Akron.

6. Akron hosts the All-American Soap Box Derby each year in August. Imagine that you have built a car to enter in the race. Either draw a picture or build a model of your car.

From *Kids on the Go* by John Haberberger • ©1994 • Teacher Ideas Press • P.O. Box 6633 • Englewood, CO 80155-6633

OKLAHOMA

Parents, have your child complete
___ questions and ___ activities.

Questions

1. Name the capital city of Oklahoma.

2. Name the states that border Oklahoma.

3. Oklahoma has an unusual shape. What do you think it looks like?

4. The word *Oklahoma* is made up of two Choctaw Indian words. What are the two words and what do they mean?

5. Oklahoma is called the Sooner State. Explain the meaning of this nickname. Who were the Sooners?

6. The United States Government originally believed that the unsettled land of Oklahoma was of little value and set it aside as "Indian Territory" in 1830. A portion of the territory was assigned to each of what the government called the Five Civilized Tribes. Name these five tribes. What does *civilized* mean? Why were these tribes called civilized?

7. Oklahoma has the second largest Native American population in the United States. Name five tribes that live in Oklahoma today.

8. Who was Will Rogers? Why is he famous?

Activities

1. Draw a map of Oklahoma. Your map should include major cities, the Will Rogers Memorial, Alabaster Caverns State Park, and Lawton.

2. Design a license plate using the Sooner State nickname.

3. Near Lawton is one of the world's largest herds of buffalo. Draw a picture of a buffalo. List the many ways that Native Americans used the buffalo. Compare a buffalo and a deer. Show how they are alike and different using the Venn diagram.

4. Oklahoma honors its Native American ancestry on the state flag. Draw a picture of the state flag and explain what the different pictures mean.

5. Make a travel brochure for the state of Oklahoma.

6. If you visited any Native American tribes and observed any ceremonies or dances, write about what you saw and learned.

From *Kids on the Go* by John Haberberger • ©1994 • Teacher Ideas Press • P.O. Box 6633 • Englewood, CO 80155-6633

OREGON

Parents, have your child complete
___ questions and ___ activities.

Questions

1. Oregon is a Pacific Northwest state. Name the states that border Oregon.

2. Name the capital city of Oregon.

3. Explain why Oregon is called the Beaver State.

4. The elevation of Oregon ranges from sea level to 11,239 feet. What is the highest point in the state?

5. Name the pioneer trail that ended in Oregon.

6. Name the two famous explorers who ended their explorations in Oregon.

7. Crater Lake is the deepest lake in the United States. Explain how Crater Lake was formed. How deep is the lake? Name the two islands in the lake.

8. Western Oregon is heavily forested and logging is a major industry in the state. Name some of the trees found in Oregon. Name five things made from wood. Predict what would happen if our forests disappeared.

Activities

1. Draw a picture of a beaver dam or lodge.

2. The Cascades, which run through Oregon, are volcanic mountains. Prepare a report on volcanoes. Draw a picture of a volcano erupting.

3. At the Bonneville Dam, on the Columbia River, there is a fish ladder. Draw a picture of the dam and the fish ladder. What is the purpose of the ladder?

4. Design a Beaver State T-shirt.

5. Draw a map of Oregon. Your map should include major cities, the Columbia River, the Cascade Mountains, Bonneville Dam, Crater Lake National Park, and Mount Hood.

6. Draw a picture of a Douglas fir tree, the Oregon state tree.

7. Make a travel brochure for the state of Oregon.

From *Kids on the Go* by John Haberberger • ©1994 • Teacher Ideas Press • P.O. Box 6633 • Englewood, CO 80155-6633

PORTLAND, OREGON

Parents, have your child complete
___ questions and ___ activities.

Questions

1. Portland is the largest city in Oregon. It is called the City of Roses. Explain why it was given that name.

2. Name the river that flows through the city. Explain the importance of the river to the city of Portland.

3. Two nearby peaks are Mount Hood and Mount St. Helens. They are in the Cascade Mountain Range. Give the elevation of the two peaks.

4. The Cascades are volcanic mountains. Explain what a volcano is. What causes it to erupt? In March of 1980 Mount St. Helens erupted. Draw pictures of the mountain before it erupted and after it erupted.

5. The Pacific Northwest is heavily forested and logging is a major industry. What different types of trees are found in these forests? Name five things made of wood. What animals depend on trees for their homes?

Activities

1. If you visit Portland in June, you might see the Rose Festival and the Grand Floral Parade. Draw a picture of your favorite float in the parade, or design a float to enter in the parade.

2. Make a travel brochure for the city of Portland.

3. Design a City of Roses T-shirt.

4. Draw a map of the Cascade Mountain Range. Label the major peaks in the range.

5. In nearby Beaverton, during the Taste of Beaverton celebration, there is a hot air balloon festival. If you saw the balloons, draw a picture of one that you liked, or design your own.

6. Keep a diary or journal of your travels or make a photo scrapbook of your trip.

PENNSYLVANIA

Parents, have your child complete
___ questions and ___ activities.

Questions

1. Name the capital city of Pennsylvania.

2. Name the largest city in the state.

3. Pennsylvania is called the Keystone State. Explain the meaning of this nickname.

4. Pennsylvania was the second of the original thirteen states to enter the Union. On what date did Pennsylvania enter the Union?

5. The Pennsylvania Dutch country is a major tourist attraction. Who are these "plain people" that make up the Pennsylvania Dutch community? From where in Europe did they come? What is special about this group of people?

6. Pennsylvania is a leader in steel production. List five things made of steel.

7. York, Pennsylvania, claims to be the first capital of the United States. Why does York makes this claim?

Activities

1. Do you like chocolate? Hershey, Pennsylvania, takes its name from M. S. Hershey, who built his chocolate factory there in 1903. The town was built around the factory. Be creative and invent a new chocolate candy bar. List the ingredients, give it a name, and draw a picture of it. Draw a magazine advertisement to sell your candy bar.

2. Draw pictures of the "plain people" that make up the Pennsylvania Dutch community. Would you want to live as they do? Why or why not?

3. Pittsburgh has been named an "all-American city." Design a T-shirt to honor Pittsburgh.

4. Draw a map of Pennsylvania. Your map should include major cities, Gettysburg, Valley Forge, Hershey, the Appalachian Mountains, York, and the Pennsylvania Dutch country.

5. Ben Franklin and his son William made an important discovery using a kite and a key during a thunderstorm. Imagine that you were there on that historic day. Design the kite that Ben used for his experiment. Either draw the kite or build a model of it.

From *Kids on the Go* by John Haberberger • ©1994 • Teacher Ideas Press • P.O. Box 6633 • Englewood, CO 80155-6633

PHILADELPHIA, PENNSYLVANIA

Parents, have your child complete
___ questions and ___ activities.

Questions

1. Name the two rivers found in Philadelphia.

2. Philadelphia is rich in the history of our nation. Independence National Historical Park is called "America's most historic square mile," with many historic sites and museums to visit. Independence Hall is the birthplace of our nation. What famous documents were adopted and signed there?

3. Christ Church is found in the park. Name three important people who attended this church in colonial times. Name the colonial leader who is buried in the Christ Church Burial Grounds.

4. The Liberty Bell Pavilion is also found in the park. The Liberty Bell is a symbol of what? Explain why the bell was rung on July 8, 1776. Explain why the bell is cracked.

5. The first U.S. Mint was in Philadelphia. What is made at a mint?

6. Philadelphia has a Tomb of the Unknown Soldier. This tomb was built in memory of whom?

7. Fairmount Park is the largest landscaped city park in the world. Compare this park with a park in your home city. Show how they are alike and different, using the Venn diagram.

8. Name the woman who is said to have made the first flag for our nation.

Activities

1. Draw a map of Independence National Historical Park. Your map should include the streets and important historical sites and museums.

2. Philadelphia is called the City of Brotherly Love. Design a T-shirt using that theme.

3. Draw a picture of the Liberty Bell.

4. Draw a picture of the first American flag.

5. Imagine that you work at the U.S. Mint and your job is to design a new two-dollar bill. Draw a picture of the bill that you design. Whose picture did you put on it?

6. Make a travel brochure for the city of Philadelphia.

From *Kids on the Go* by John Haberberger • ©1994 • Teacher Ideas Press • P.O. Box 6633 • Englewood, CO 80155-6633

RHODE ISLAND

Parents, have your child complete
___ questions and ___ activities.

Questions

1. Name the capital city of Rhode Island.

2. The state of Rhode Island has an official title. What is it?

3. An island is a body of land completely surrounded by water. Does the state of Rhode Island fit this definition? Why do you think the state is called Rhode Island?

4. Name the white settler who founded Rhode Island. Explain why he left Massachusetts and bought land in what is now Rhode Island.

5. Explain why Roger Williams chose the name Providence for the town that he founded.

6. Rhode Island may be the nation's smallest state, but it is a state of many firsts. Rhode Island was the first state to proclaim independence from Great Britain, two months before the Declaration of Independence was signed. On what date did Rhode Island declare its independence? What is the Declaration of Independence?

7. Explain how Cow Cove on Block Island got its unusual name.

Activities

1. The state bird is the Rhode Island red hen. Draw a picture of this bird.

2. The Rhode Island Red character is seen in Bugs Bunny cartoons. Create a comic strip using the Rhode Island Red and some of the other characters from that cartoon show.

3. Draw a map of Rhode Island. Your map should include major cities, the islands near the mainland, Cow Cove, Arcadia State Park, and Scituate Reservoir.

4. Newport is famous as a summer resort. The wealthy people who continue to visit Newport sometimes have outrageous social events. Parties have been given for dogs, and one was even held for a monkey. Pretend that you are having a birthday party for your pet. Write a guest list of the people and animals that will attend, tell about the activities that will go on at the party, and make a sample of the invitation that you will send to the guests.

5. A statewide annual event is the May Breakfasts. This started in 1867 and features many Rhode Island favorite foods. One of the favorites is jonnycakes. What are jonnycakes? Write the recipe for them. Make some jonnycakes and serve them to the class when you return.

From *Kids on the Go* by John Haberberger • ©1994 • Teacher Ideas Press • P.O. Box 6633 • Englewood, CO 80155-6633

SOUTH CAROLINA

Parents, have your child complete
___ questions and ___ activities.

Questions

1. Name the capital city of South Carolina.

2. For whom was South Carolina named? Name the states that border South Carolina.

4. South Carolina was the first state to secede from the Union. What does *secede* mean and why did South Carolina do that?

5. Charleston was the first permanent English settlement in South Carolina. What was Charleston first called?

6. At Patriots Point Naval and Maritime Museum, near Charleston, naval vessels are open for tours. Name the ships moored at the museum. Write about one new thing you learned if you toured the museum.

7. The South Carolina state beverage is milk. Explain why milk is important for your body. List five dairy products.

8. What is the name of the large island on the southeast coast of South Carolina that is such a popular recreation area?

9. South Carolina is a major producer of cotton. What is cotton? Write a list of five things made from cotton.

Activities

1. If you visited Patriots Point Museum draw pictures of the vessels you saw and label each picture.

2. The South Carolina State dance is the shag. Learn how to do this dance and demonstrate it to the class. You could also teach the class how to do it.

3. The South Carolina State reptile is the loggerhead turtle. Draw a picture of this turtle. Compare this turtle with a box turtle. Show how they are alike and different, using the Venn diagram.

4. The Atlantic Ocean is considered South Carolina's greatest natural asset. The beaches are perfect for many activities. If you went to a beach, give the name of it and write about what you saw and did there.

5. Draw a map of South Carolina. Your map should include major cities, Charleston, Andrew Jackson State Park, Hilton Head, the Savannah River, and the Atlantic Ocean.

6. Gullah is a curious-sounding language spoken by a group of African Americans who inhabit the sea islands and coastal regions of South Carolina, Georgia, and northeastern Florida. If you heard this language, learn some words that you could teach the class when you return.

From *Kids on the Go* by John Haberberger • ©1994 • Teacher Ideas Press • P.O. Box 6633 • Englewood, CO 80155-6633

SOUTH DAKOTA

Parents, have your child complete
___ questions and ___ activities.

Questions

1. Name the capital city of South Dakota.

2. South Dakota has two nicknames, Coyote State and Sunshine State. Explain the meanings of these two names. What is a coyote?

3. Badlands National Park is found near Rapid City. If you visited the park, draw a picture of what you saw. Explain how the Badlands were formed.

4. When completed, the Crazy Horse Memorial near Custer will be the world's largest statue. It will depict Crazy Horse riding a magnificent horse. Prepare a report about Crazy Horse and explain why he was important.

5. Wild Bill Hickok was shot and killed in Deadwood. Who was Wild Bill and why was he important in the history of the West?

6. Near Rapid City is the Mount Rushmore National Memorial. Name the four American presidents whose faces are carved in this mountain in the Black Hills. Name the sculptor who began the project and the sculptor who completed it.

Activities

1. Draw a map of South Dakota. Your map should include major cities, Deadwood, Rapid City and Mount Rushmore, Custer National Forest, Custer, the Black Hills, Badlands National Park, and the Missouri River.

2. Draw a picture of Mount Rushmore.

3. The Mammoth Site of Hot Springs is known for being the graveyard for what prehistoric animals? In 1984 the world's sixth Tyrannosaurus Rex was discovered there. Draw a picture of Tyrannosaurus Rex.

4. Draw a picture of the Crazy Horse Memorial statue.

5. Wind Cave National Park is one of the largest caves in the world. How did the park get its name? Underground are limestone crystal formations. What is limestone? If you took a tour of the cave, draw a picture of what you saw.

6. Make a travel brochure for the state of South Dakota.

From *Kids on the Go* by John Haberberger • ©1994 • Teacher Ideas Press • P.O. Box 6633 • Englewood, CO 80155-6633

TENNESSEE

Parents, have your child complete
___ questions and ___ activities.

Questions

1. Name the capital city of Tennessee.

2. Explain why Tennessee is called the Volunteer State. What is a volunteer?

3. If you climb Lookout Mountain, near Chattanooga, on a clear day, you have an unobstructed view all around. List the neighboring states that you can see.

4. Great Smoky Mountains National Park, half in Tennessee and half in North Carolina, is the country's most visited national park. Which mountain range is older, the Rocky Mountains or the Great Smokies? Explain how the Great Smokies got their name.

5. Tell who named the city of Memphis and what the word means.

6. Memphis is known as the cotton center of the world. List five things made of cotton.

Activities

1. List five things that you can volunteer to do. Design a volunteer T-shirt for yourself.

2. Draw a map of Tennessee. Your map should include major cities, the Great Smoky Mountains, the Chisholm Trail, Chattanooga and Lookout Mountain, and the Tennessee River.

3. If you visited the Great Smokies, you may have seen a bear. Draw pictures of two species of bear and identify them.

4. Draw a picture of a cotton plant. List the steps needed to turn harvested cotton into material to make clothing. You could draw pictures to show the steps in the process.

5. Chattanooga is the birthplace of miniature golf. Do you like to play miniature golf? Be creative and design a nine- or eighteen-hole miniature golf course.

6. Make a travel brochure for the state of Tennessee.

From *Kids on the Go* by John Haberberger • ©1994 • Teacher Ideas Press • P.O. Box 6633 • Englewood, CO 80155-6633

TEXAS

Parents, have your child complete
___ questions and ___ activities.

Questions

1. Name the capital city of Texas. For whom was it named?

2. Name the largest city in the state.

3. Texas was once the largest state in our nation. Name the state that is larger than Texas.

4. Tell why Texas is called the Lone Star State.

5. Texas is in two time zones. Name the two zones. Tell what happens when you travel from one time zone to another. What must you do to your watch? Explain why there are different time zones across the United States.

6. The battle at the Alamo was important in the history of Texas. Explain what happened in this famous battle. The Alamo was a Spanish mission. What was the name of the mission?

7. On what date did Texas join the Union?

8. Write a paragraph telling who shouted "Remember the Alamo," when it was said, and what was happening at the time.

Activities

1. Design a Lone Star T-shirt.

2. Draw a map of the state of Texas. Your map should include major cities, Big Bend National Park, San Antonio and the Alamo, Padre Island, the Colorado River, and the Rio Grande River.

3. Draw a picture of the Alamo.

4. The bones of a prehistoric Pterodactyl were found at Big Bend National Park. What was a Pterodactyl? Draw a picture of one.

5. Chili became the state dish in 1977. Do you like chili? Be creative and invent a chili recipe. List the ingredients and write the recipe.

6. How far can you spit a watermelon seed? In Luling at the Great Watermelon Thump there is a contest to see who can spit one the farthest. Organize a seed-spitting contest for your family. What prize will the winner get?

7. Plan a Texas vacation for your family. It will be a two-week vacation and you will travel by car. List the places you will visit. Also figure the total number of miles you will travel.

From *Kids on the Go* by John Haberberger • ©1994 • Teacher Ideas Press • P.O. Box 6633 • Englewood, CO 80155-6633

DALLAS/FORT WORTH, TEXAS

Parents, have your child complete
___ questions and ___ activities.

Questions

1. The Dallas/Fort Worth Metroplex is located in which part of Texas?

2. List ten of the cities in the Metroplex in alphabetical order. How many people live in the Metroplex?

3. Who was the first settler of the area?

4. The Dallas Zoo reptile house has one of the world's largest rattlesnake collections. What is a reptile? Name five animals that are reptiles.

5. The sixth floor of the Texas School Book Depository is a memorial to the late President John F. Kennedy. If you visited the memorial, describe what you saw there. Write about something you learned from your visit.

6. The Reunion Tower is a modern Dallas landmark. What is the historical significance of the tower? Draw a picture of the tower.

7. Give the name of the general for whom Fort Worth was named.

8. If you visited Six Flags Over Texas, in nearby Arlington, describe your favorite ride.

Activities

1. Build a model or draw a picture of the cabin built by the first settler in the Dallas area.

2. Prepare a report on rattlesnakes. Your report should tell about the different types of rattlesnakes and where they are found. Include pictures in your report.

3. Use your imagination and create a new ride for Six Flags Over Texas. Draw a picture of your ride and explain what it does.

4. Do you like football? Are you a Dallas Cowboys fan? Design a jersey for the Cowboys.

5. At Glen Rose, a Metroplex city, is the Dinosaur Valley State Park. The park has the best-preserved dinosaur tracks in Texas. Name the dinosaurs that left these tracks and draw pictures of the dinosaurs and their tracks.

6. Make a travel brochure for the Dallas/Fort Worth Metroplex.

From *Kids on the Go* by John Haberberger • ©1994 • Teacher Ideas Press • P.O. Box 6633 • Englewood, CO 80155-6633

HOUSTON, TEXAS

Parents, have your child complete
___ questions and ___ activities.

Questions

1. Houston, the largest city in Texas, is located in which part of the state? It is near which body of water?

2. Houston is named after a Texas army general. What was his full name?

3. Houston was founded in 1836. Name the two brothers who founded the city.

4. Astroworld/Waterworld is one of the nation's great amusement centers. If you visited the center, write about what you saw there. What was your favorite thing to do?

5. The Lyndon B. Johnson Space Center is the headquarters of America's manned space program. If you visited the center, prepare a report that explains what it is and what work is done there. Who was Lyndon B. Johnson and why was the center named for him?

6. The Orange Show is a bizarre attraction of many things. If you went to the show, write a paragraph describing it and naming some of the things found there.

Activities

1. Use your imagination to create a new ride or attraction for Astroworld/Waterworld. Draw a picture of your idea and explain what it does or how it works.

2. Build a model of a rocket to show the class. Explain what powers your rocket. Write about the rockets used in today's space program.

3. Do you think that there is life on other planets? Draw a picture of how you think alien creatures might look. Write a one-paragraph description of the creature that you drew.

4. If you saw the Orange Show, create your own show of oddities. Either draw pictures or build models of your unusual things.

5. The Houston Astrodome has been called the eighth wonder of the world. Draw a picture of the Astrodome. List the Seven Wonders of the World.

6. Are you a Houston Oilers fan? Design a Houston Oilers jersey.

From *Kids on the Go* by John Haberberger • ©1994 • Teacher Ideas Press • P.O. Box 6633 • Englewood, CO 80155-6633

UTAH

Parents, have your child complete
___ questions and ___ activities.

Questions

1. What is the capital city of Utah?

2. Utah is called the Beehive State. Explain why it has this nickname.

3. Utah is a western state. Name the states that border Utah.

4. Utah takes its name from which group of Native Americans?

5. Name the religious group that permanently settled the wilderness land that is now Utah. Who was their leader?

6. An important landmark in Utah is the Great Salt Lake near Salt Lake City. How was the lake formed? Explain why the lake is saltier than the oceans.

7. The area at Dinosaur National Monument has provided more skeletons, skulls, and bones of Jurassic period dinosaurs than any other dig in the world. How long ago was the Jurassic period? Name some of the dinosaurs from that period.

8. Natural Bridges National Monument features three natural bridges, all with Hopi Indian names. Give the names of the three bridges.

Activities

1. Design a Beehive State T-shirt.

2. Draw a map of Utah. Your map should include major cities, Bryce Canyon National Park, the Great Salt Lake, and Promontory Summit.

3. In Bingham is the largest open-pit copper mine in North America. The mine is also the biggest hole in the ground in the world. How deep is the hole? How far across is it? Draw a picture of the hole. List five things made of copper.

4. The Union Pacific and Central Pacific railroads joined at Promontory Summit in 1869. This completed the first transcontinental railroad in the United States. What does *transcontinental* mean? Why were railroads so important in the late 1800s in the United States? Draw pictures of an early train locomotive and a present-day train engine. Show how they are alike and different, using the Venn diagram.

5. Keep a diary or journal of your travels in Utah or make a photo scrapbook of your trip.

From *Kids on the Go* by John Haberberger • ©1994 • Teacher Ideas Press • P.O. Box 6633 • Englewood, CO 80155-6633

SALT LAKE CITY, UTAH

Parents, have your child complete
___ questions and ___ activities.

Questions

1. Name the settlers who built Salt Lake City.

2. Near the state capitol building is Temple Square with the famed Mormon Temple and Tabernacle. The Tabernacle is where the Mormon Tabernacle Choir sings. The acoustics are excellent in this building. What are acoustics? Why do you think the acoustics are so good in the Tabernacle?

3. West of the city is the Great Salt Lake. How deep is the lake? Explain why the lake is twice as salty as the ocean. Explain why humans cannot sink in the water.

4. The Wheeler Historic Farm shows what farm life was like around 1900. If you visited this farm, prepare a report that tells about the farm and one new thing that you learned.

5. Name the mountains that are just east of the city. There are many ski areas close by, and skiing in Utah is popular because of the powder snow. Explain why powder snow is so light and fluffy.

6. Would you want to live in Salt Lake City? Write your answer and tell why or why not.

Activities

1. Utah is called the Beehive State. Draw a picture or make a model of a beehive. Explain how a beehive is made.

2. Draw pictures of the Mormon Temple and Tabernacle.

3. Did you get to listen to the Tabernacle choir? If you have a tape of the choir, share it with the class when you return.

4. If you visited the Wheeler Historic Farm, draw a picture of how the farm looked. Your picture should include the farmhouse, other buildings, and animals.

5. Salt Lake City was laid out in a grid fashion. What is a grid? Draw a map of the city. Your map should include Temple Square, the Temple, the Tabernacle, the Brigham Young Monument, and the state capitol building. Remember to include the streets and their names.

6. Make a travel brochure for Salt Lake City.

From *Kids on the Go* by John Haberberger • ©1994 • Teacher Ideas Press • P.O. Box 6633 • Englewood, CO 80155-6633

VERMONT

Parents, have your child complete
___ questions and ___ activities.

Questions

1. Name the capital city of Vermont.

2. Name the largest city in the state.

3. Name the oldest city in the state.

4. At Bennington is the Bennington Battle Monument, a granite tower that is 302 feet high. What happened in the Bennington battle? Why was it important to the Americans?

5. Explain why Vermont is called the Green Mountain State.

6. The Crowley Cheese Factory, in Ludlow, is the oldest cheese factory in the United States. If you visited the town and the factory, explain how cheese is made. Draw pictures showing the steps in the process. List five dairy products.

7. Vermont was the fourteenth state to enter the Union. On what date did Vermont enter the Union?

8. Barre is home to the world's largest granite quarries. Vermont also has marble quarries and mines, and at Proctor is the Vermont Marble Exhibit. What is granite? What is marble? What is a quarry?

Activities

1. Draw a map of Vermont. Your map should include major cities, the towns of Stowe and Vergennes, the Green Mountain National Park, the Long Trail, the Green Mountains, Bennington, and Lake Champlain.

2. The 260-mile Long Trail, a popular hiking route, extends the length of the state. Plan a backpacking trip for your family on this trail. You should indicate where you will begin and end your trip, where you will be camping each night, and how many days the trip will last.

3. Design a Green Mountain State T-shirt.

4. Lake Memphremagog, a deep glacial lake at Newport, is home to a large creature similar to the Loch Ness Monster. Like the Loch Ness Monster this creature, called Memphre, has rarely been sighted. Draw a picture of what you think Memphre looks like.

5. Bellows Falls has a distribution center for Ben & Jerry's Ice Cream. Be creative and invent a new flavor for Ben & Jerry.

From *Kids on the Go* by John Haberberger • ©1994 • Teacher Ideas Press • P.O. Box 6633 • Englewood, CO 80155-6633

VIRGINIA

Parents, have your child complete
___ questions and ___ activities.

Questions

1. Name the capital city of Virginia.

2. Virginia was settled by Elizabethans. For whom did they name their settlement?

3. Name the states that border Virginia.

4. Virginia has the nickname Old Dominion. Explain the meaning of this name.

5. The first permanent English settlement in the New World was Jamestown. When was it founded? Name the ships that brought the settlers to Jamestown. Who was the leader of the group?

6. The Great Dismal Swamp, near Norfolk, is made up of layers of peat. What is peat? Near the center of the swamp is Lake Drummond, a lake of juniper water. What is juniper water? What is special about this water? How was it used by sailors?

7. The Pentagon, the world's largest office building, is located in Arlington. How many sides does a pentagon have? Draw a picture of a pentagon. Who works at the Pentagon?

8. The Colonial Williamsburg area is a restoration project of the city of Williamsburg. What is the meaning of *restoration*? Who started this project. Explain why it is important to preserve history.

Activities

1. Draw pictures of the three ships that brought the settlers to Jamestown and name each ship.

2. If you visited the Great Dismal Swamp, draw a picture of the swamp. Your picture should include wildlife and trees found there.

3. If you visited George Washington's home, Mount Vernon, draw a picture of it. Draw a picture of your home and compare the two. Show how they are alike and different, using the Venn diagram.

4. Records show that America's first Thanksgiving was held December 4, 1619, in Berkeley, Virginia. Draw a picture of the first Thanksgiving feast. List the foods the Pilgrims may have eaten and the activities they may have organized for that day.

5. Part of the Blue Ridge Parkway is in Virginia. Plan an auto trip on the parkway. Name the towns you will visit. Tell how many miles you will drive.

6. Draw a map of Virginia. Your map should include major cities, Jamestown, Arlington, Williamsburg, the Blue Ridge Mountains, and the Blue Ridge Parkway.

7. Prepare a report on the rich colonial history of Williamsburg.

8. If you visited Colonial Williamsburg, draw pictures of a boy and girl dressed in eighteenth-century clothes.

From *Kids on the Go* by John Haberberger • ©1994 • Teacher Ideas Press • P.O. Box 6633 • Englewood, CO 80155-6633

WASHINGTON

Parents, have your child complete
___ questions and ___ activities.

Questions

1. Name the capital city of Washington.

2. Why is Washington called the Evergreen State?

3. The elevation of Washington ranges from sea level to 14,410 feet. What is the highest point in the state?

4. The mighty Columbia River flows through Washington. Captain Robert Gray named the river in 1792. Explain why he chose the name Columbia for the river.

5. Washington grows more apples than any place in the world. Where in the state are the apple orchards found? List five different varieties of apples.

6. Rich forests are found in Washington and logging is a major industry. Name five things made from wood. Name five animals that use trees for their homes. Predict what would happen if our forests disappeared.

Activities

1. Mount Rainier, which is dormant, is the largest volcano in the Cascade range. What is the meaning of *dormant*? Mount St. Helens, the youngest volcano in the range, erupted on March 27, 1980. Draw pictures of Mount St. Helens before and after it erupted. Prepare a report on volcanoes.

2. Design a license plate using the Evergreen State nickname.

3. Draw a map of Washington. Your map should include major cities, the Columbia River with the Grand Coulee Dam, Mount Rainier, Mount St. Helens, the Olympic Mountains, Puget Sound, and the San Juan Islands.

4. The Grand Coulee Dam on the Columbia is one of the largest concrete structures in the world. Prepare a report on the dam, giving facts about it and explaining its importance to the state of Washington. Draw a picture of the dam.

5. Many totem poles are found in Washington. They were carved by the Pacific Northwest Indians. What is a totem pole? Make a totem pole or draw a picture of one.

From *Kids on the Go* by John Haberberger • ©1994 • Teacher Ideas Press • P.O. Box 6633 • Englewood, CO 80155-6633

SEATTLE, WASHINGTON

Parents, have your child complete
___ questions and ___ activities.

Questions

1. Seattle is located next to which body of salt water?

2. Explain why Seattle is called the Emerald City. What is an emerald?

3. Seattle was built on seven hills. What is the elevation of Seattle?

4. Name the mountain ranges on both sides of Seattle.

5. Seattle was named for an Indian chief. What was his name?

6. The landmark of the city is the Space Needle. How high is the needle? Where is it located? Explain why the needle was built.

7. On Puget Sound you will find many ferryboats. If you rode one, write about your trip. Tell where you went and describe the ride. How much did it cost for your family to ride the boat?

8. Seattle has two floating bridges. Explain why they are able to "float." Compare a floating bridge with another bridge that you have seen. Show how they are alike and different, using the Venn diagram.

9. At the Pike Place Market you will find many shops. If you visited the market, write about what you saw there. What was the most interesting thing that you saw?

Activities

1. Draw a picture or build a model of the Space Needle.

2. Imagine that you have a shop at the Pike Place Market. What do you sell in your shop? Draw a magazine advertisement for your shop.

3. Make a travel brochure for the city of Seattle.

4. If you visited the Government Locks, prepare a report about them. Explain their purpose and how they work.

5. Draw a picture of a floating bridge.

6. Design an Emerald City T-shirt for Seattle.

From *Kids on the Go* by John Haberberger • ©1994 • Teacher Ideas Press • P.O. Box 6633 • Englewood, CO 80155-6633

WASHINGTON, DC

Parents, have your child complete
___ questions and ___ activities.

Questions

1. The city of Washington and the District of Columbia are the same. The District is nestled between which two states?

2. Name the man who designed Washington.

3. In what year did Washington become the nation's capital?

4. Name the two rivers that flow through Washington.

5. The U.S. Capitol Building is where the laws of the nation are made. Name the two houses of Congress. Do you think laws are important? What might happen in our country if we had no laws.

6. There are many memorials in Washington, DC. What is the reason for a memorial? Do you think they are important? Write why or why not and make a list of the memorials in the city.

7. The Smithsonian Institution is the world's largest museum complex. For whom is it named? How many museums are in the complex?

8. The White House is where our presidents live. Why is the president given such a large, elegant house in which to live?

Activities

1. In the Smithsonian's Museum of Natural History is a dinosaur egg that is 70 million years old. What could be inside? Use your imagination and write a short story about what happens when the egg cracks open.

2. Make up a new law that you think would benefit our country.

3. Draw a picture of the White House.

4. Draw a map of Washington, DC. Your map should include the White House, the Capitol Building, the Washington Monument, the Lincoln Memorial, the Reflecting Pool, and the Smithsonian Institution. Remember to draw the streets and name them.

5. Design a Washington, DC T-shirt.

6. Compare your house and the White House. Show how they are alike and different, using the Venn diagram.

7. Design a walking tour of Washington, DC. Write the plan for your tour, describing the things that the visitor will see.

8. Draw a map showing Washington, DC and the states that border the District of Columbia. Your map should name these states.

From *Kids on the Go* by John Haberberger • ©1994 • Teacher Ideas Press • P.O. Box 6633 • Englewood, CO 80155-6633

WEST VIRGINIA

Parents, have your child complete
___ questions and ___ activities.

Questions

1. Name the capital city of West Virginia.

2. The region that is now West Virginia was first inhabited by the Mound Builders. Who were these Mound Builders? Why do you think they built the mounds? What is inside the mounds?

3. What important historical event happened at Point Pleasant?

4. Explain why West Virginia is called the Mountain State.

5. Virginia and West Virginia used to be one, called the Commonwealth of Virginia. Explain why the counties in what is now West Virginia formed their own state. Give the date that West Virginia entered the Union.

6. At the National Radio Astronomy Observatory, in Marlington, scientists study the universe using radio telescopes. What is a radio telescope? Would you want to be an astronomer? Write why or why not.

7. The New River Gorge Bridge, at Gauley Bridge, is the world's largest steel span bridge. Name the river that flows through the canyon. How high above the river is the bridge?

Activities

1. If you saw the earth mounds built by the Mound Builders, draw pictures of five different mounds.

2. The West Virginia state animal is the black bear. Draw pictures of the black bear and one other type of bear. Compare the two bears. Show how they are alike and different, using the Venn diagram.

3. If you saw the New River Gorge Bridge, draw a picture of it.

4. If you visited the National Radio Astronomy Observatory, prepare a report on it. Explain the work that is done there and tell of one new thing that you learned. Draw a picture of the night sky with the Big Dipper.

5. Draw a map of West Virginia. Your map should include major cities, the New River Gorge National River Park, Point Pleasant, Blackwater Falls State Park, and the Appalachian Mountains.

6. At the New River Gorge Bridge, parachutists are allowed to jump off the bridge on Bridge Day in October. Imagine that you are going to jump and draw a picture of your parachute.

From *Kids on the Go* by John Haberberger • ©1994 • Teacher Ideas Press • P.O. Box 6633 • Englewood, CO 80155-6633

WISCONSIN

Parents, have your child complete
___ questions and ___ activities.

Questions

1. Name the capital city of Wisconsin.

2. Explain how Wisconsin got the nickname Badger State.

3. Native Americans called the land *Ouisconsin*. What is the meaning of the word? Is it an appropriate name for Wisconsin?

4. Explain why Wisconsin is called America's dairyland. List five dairy products.

5. The state tree is the sugar maple. What food do we get from maple trees?

6. Explain why Wisconsin is a popular place for those who enjoy fishing. Name the largest freshwater lake in the state.

7. Madison is called the City of Four Lakes. What are the names of the four lakes?

8. Native Americans called the Milwaukee area *Millioki*. What is the meaning of that word?

9. "The farmer in the dell" may have been in Wisconsin Dells, the state's prime tourist attraction. What is a dell? Draw a picture of a dell.

Activities

1. Reedsburg calls itself the Butter Capital of America. If you visited the Wisconsin Dairies plant, explain how butter is made. You could draw pictures to show the steps in the process.

2. Baraboo is the original home of the Ringling Brothers of circus fame. Imagine that you are a circus clown and design a clown face for yourself.

3. Wisconsin's great paper industry started in Neenah-Menasha, where many paper product factories are located. Explain how paper is made. You could draw pictures to show the steps in the process.

4. Draw a map of Wisconsin. Your map should include major cities, the Mississippi River, Lake Superior, Lake Michigan, Green Bay, Wisconsin Dells, the Wisconsin River, Baraboo, and Oshkosh.

5. At Boulder Junction the fishing for muskellunge is excellent. Draw a picture of this fish.

6. Oshkosh is a popular brand of clothing. Design a Badger State T-shirt for Oshkosh to make.

WYOMING

Parents, have your child complete
___ questions and ___ activities.

Questions

1. Name the capital city of Wyoming.

2. Wyoming is called the Cowboy State and the bucking horse insignia has appeared on Wyoming license plates for many years. Why is the cowboy such an important symbol of this state?

3. A major attraction in Wyoming is Yellowstone National Park, which is our nation's oldest national park. In what year did the U.S. Congress make it a national park? Why is it called Yellowstone?

4. The world's most famous geyser, Old Faithful, is found in Yellowstone. Why is it called Old Faithful? Explain what causes geysers to erupt.

5. Millions of years ago southwestern Wyoming was under water, and today fossils of the prehistoric water creatures can be found. What are some of the fossils that can be seen in the rocks in that area?

6. River waters generally flow to the east or west of the Continental Divide. What is unusual about the waters of the Great Divide Basin?

7. The Wyoming Territorial Park in Laramie gives visitors the opportunity to experience what life was like in the 1800s. The Wyoming Territorial Prison was "home" for many notorious outlaws. Name some of the infamous prisoners that were kept at the prison. Make a wanted poster for one of the prisoners.

Activities

1. Design a license plate for Wyoming.

2. Draw pictures of the dinosaurs and other animals that lived in prehistoric Wyoming.

3. If you visited the Territorial Park in Laramie, write about what you saw and learned. Draw pictures of a man and a woman dressed as they looked in pioneer times. Would you have wanted to live during those early days in the West? Explain why or why not.

4. Draw a map of Wyoming. Your map should include major cities, the Rocky Mountains, the Great Divide Basin, Yellowstone National Park, and Grand Teton National Park.

5. Make a travel brochure for the state of Wyoming.

YELLOWSTONE NATIONAL PARK, WYOMING

Parents, have your child complete
___ questions and ___ activities.

Questions

1. Yellowstone was the world's first national park. In what year did the U.S. Congress establish this wilderness as a national park?

2. Yellowstone is home to many species of mammals, birds, and fish. Write a list of five animals that you saw there.

3. The rodents that live in the park are an important part of the food chain in Yellowstone. What is a *food chain*? Write the definition of the term. Predict what would happen to the larger animals if there were no rodents.

4. Write a paragraph explaining why park visitors should not feed or disturb any wild animals.

5. The world's largest area of geyser activity is found at Yellowstone. What is a geyser?

6. The Norris Geyser Basin is the most exciting thermal area in the park. What does *thermal* mean? Write the names of five geysers found in this basin.

7. Old Faithful is the world's most famous geyser. Explain why it is named Old Faithful.

Activities

1. Draw a map of the park. Your map should include the Grand Loop Road, Old Faithful, the Norris Geyser Basin, West Thumb, and Yellowstone Lake.

2. Draw a picture of an animal you saw in its natural setting.

3. The black bear and grizzly bear both live in the park. Using the Venn diagram show how the bears are alike and different. Draw pictures of both bears.

4. Prepare a report on geysers. Your report should explain the cause of geyser activity.

5. Draw a picture of a geyser erupting.

6. Make a travel brochure for Yellowstone National Park.

FOREIGN TRAVEL

FOREIGN TRAVEL

Parents, have your child complete
___ questions and ___ activities.

Questions

1. Which foreign country did you visit? On which continent is the country? Name the neighbors of the country you visited.

2. What does *foreign* mean? Were you an alien when you visited the foreign country? If you were, explain why.

3. Describe where you stayed in the country. Was it a hotel, a hostel, a kibbutz?

4. What currency is used in the country? Give the names and values of some of the coins and bills.

5. Some countries have special events and attractions for visitors to enjoy. Write about any special attraction or museum you visited or event you attended.

6. List five animals found in the country you visited.

7. What are some of the foods native to the country? Did you enjoy the local food? Explain why or why not. Compare the evening meal in the country you visited with the evening meal at your home. Show how they are alike and different, using the Venn diagram.

8. Name the sports played in the country.

9. What are some of the customs of the country?

Activities

1. Draw a map of the country you visited. Your map should include the capital city, other important cities, important rivers and seaports, and any special geographical landmarks.

2. Draw a picture of the flag of the country.

3. Draw pictures of a boy and a girl dressed in traditional costumes of the country.

4. Plan a dinner menu for your family using foods from the country.

5. Draw pictures of the animals you saw in the country.

6. If you brought any souvenirs or crafts back from your visit, share them with the class when you return.

7. Keep a diary or journal of your travels or make a photo scrapbook of your trip.

From *Kids on the Go* by John Haberberger • ©1994 • Teacher Ideas Press • P.O. Box 6633 • Englewood, CO 80155-6633

WAYS TO TRAVEL

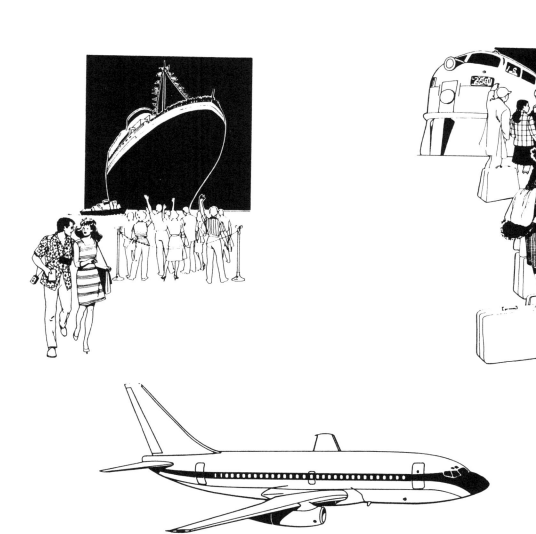

AIRPLANE

1. Describe the aircraft in which you flew. Give the name and model number of the plane. What color was it? How many engines did the plane have and where were they located? What type of fuel was used? How many passengers did the plane carry? Draw a picture of the plane.

2. How many people made up the crew of the plane? Name the different jobs and describe them.

3. At what altitude did the plane fly? How fast did it fly? How long did the flight take? Was it a nonstop flight? If not, in what cities did you stop?

4. Did the plane fly through any time zones? If so, tell what happened. Did you experience jet lag? What is jet lag?

5. If you flew to another country, did you fly over an ocean? If so, tell which ocean.

6. How much did it cost for your family to fly?

7. Explain the differences between flying first class and flying coach.

8. Was this your first flight? If so, describe the feelings you had.

From *Kids on the Go* by John Haberberger • ©1994 • Teacher Ideas Press • P.O. Box 6633 • Englewood, CO 80155-6633

AUTOMOBILE

1. Describe the vehicle in which you traveled. Was it a sedan, station wagon, van? Draw a picture of the vehicle.

2. Through which states or countries did you travel? In which direction did you travel? Draw a map of your trip.

3. How many miles was it to your destination? How long did it take to reach your destination? What was the average speed?

4. Explain what you did in the car while traveling. If you stopped at night, where did you stay? If you ate at restaurants, did you try any new foods? If so, describe them.

5. Figure the gas mileage for the trip and the amount of money spent on fuel.

BUS

1. Describe the bus on which you traveled. How many passengers did the bus carry? Did the bus have bathrooms? Draw a picture of the bus.

2. Is a special license required to drive a bus? If so, what kind?

3. Where did you board the bus in your home city? If it was a bus station, describe it.

4. In which direction did you travel? Which states did you travel through? How many miles did you travel to reach your destination? How long did it take to reach your destination? What did you do while on the road? Write about any stops the bus made; tell where they were and what you did.

5. How much did it cost for your family to ride on the bus?

6. Compare a bus and a car. Show how they are alike and different, using the Venn diagram.

7. Did you enjoy traveling by bus? Explain why or why not.

From *Kids on the Go* by John Haberberger • ©1994 • Teacher Ideas Press • P.O. Box 6633 • Englewood, CO 80155-6633

SHIP

1. Describe the ship on which you traveled. Give the name of the ship. How long was the ship? How many decks did it have? What did you find on the different decks? What type of engines did the ship have? Draw a picture of the ship.

2. Explain how a ship moves through the water. How fast can it go?

3. If you were able to visit the wheelhouse and meet the captain, tell what he does to command the ship. What are his responsibilities? What is another word for *wheelhouse*?

4. How many people made up the crew of the ship? Name five different jobs and describe them.

5. A cruise ship offers many activities for the passengers. What are some things that you did? If you did not travel on a cruise ship, what type of ship was it? How much did it cost for your family to travel on the ship?

6. Over which ocean or body of water did you travel? How long did the voyage take?

7. Choose one of the decks and draw a picture of it.

From *Kids on the Go* by John Haberberger • ©1994 • Teacher Ideas Press • P.O. Box 6633 • Englewood, CO 80155-6633

TRAIN

1. Describe the train on which you traveled. How many cars made up the train? How many engines did it have? What kind of motors were used? How many passengers were on the train? Did the train have a caboose? Why is a caboose needed? Draw a picture of the train.

2. How many people made up the crew of the train? Name the different jobs and describe them. If you were able to meet the engineer, write about what he does to operate the train and what his responsibilities are.

3. Train tracks are parallel. What does *parallel* mean? Name other things that are parallel.

4. In which direction did you travel? Through which states or countries did you travel?

5. How many miles was it to your destination? What was the speed of the train? How long did the trip take? Did you sleep overnight on the train? If so, describe what it was like. How was the food on the train?

6. How much did it cost for your family to travel by train?

7. Was this your first train trip? Did you enjoy the trip?

From *Kids on the Go* by John Haberberger • ©1994 • Teacher Ideas Press • P.O. Box 6633 • Englewood, CO 80155-6633

FIELD TRIPS

AIRPORT

Questions

1. What is the name of the airport you visited?
2. The airport has a large building called a terminal. What is a terminal?
3. How many gates does the terminal have?
4. Make a list of the concessions or stores found in the terminal.
5. Explain why passengers must pass through a security check before they can board the aircraft.
6. Explain how a runway is built. Why must a runway be so thick?
7. How long is a runway? Name something that is long like a runway.
8. How many runways does the airport have? In which direction do they run?
9. What is de-icing? Explain why it is important for a plane to be de-iced.
10. What is the control tower? What is the air traffic controller's job? Why is it so important?

Activities

1. Draw an aerial view of the airport. Your picture should include the terminal building, the runways, and any maintenance facilities.
2. Build a model of the airport.
3. Choose an airline company that uses the airport and create an advertisement for the company.
4. Compare an airplane with a bird. Show how they are alike and different, using the Venn diagram.
5. Compare an early aircraft with a modern plane. Show how they are alike and different, using the Venn diagram.
6. Build a model airplane.

From *Kids on the Go* by John Haberberger • ©1994 • Teacher Ideas Press • P.O. Box 6633 • Englewood, CO 80155-6633

ART MUSEUM

Questions

1. Name the art museum you visited.

2. An art museum is a place to look at and think about art objects. Write a paragraph that shares some of your thoughts as you toured the museum.

3. Do you think that an art museum is important? Explain why or why not.

4. Predict what might happen if there were no art museums.

5. What was the largest thing you saw in the museum?

6. What was the smallest thing you saw?

7. What was the most colorful thing you saw?

8. Write about one new thing that you learned from your visit to the museum.

9. Compare the art museum with another museum that you have visited. Show how they are alike and different, using the Venn diagram.

10. What did you like best and least about the art museum? Explain your answers.

Activities

1. Draw a picture of an art object you liked, color it, and cut it into a puzzle. See if a friend can put it together.

2. People react to art when they see it. Think of something you saw that was "awesome." Draw a picture of it, and write one paragraph to describe it.

3. If you learned about a famous artist, pretend that you are that artist. Create something in the style of that artist.

4. Choose a painting that you saw and pretend that you are in the painting. What is it like living in a painting? Create a story telling how you got there and what adventures you had.

5. Choose two paintings or objects by the same artist and compare them. Show how they are alike and different, using the Venn diagram.

6. Research an artist and explain how or why the artist created a certain work of art. What was the artist's idea or inspiration for the work?

BOTANICAL GARDENS

Questions

1. Name five things that you saw at the gardens.

2. Did the gardens have a conservatory? What is a conservatory? What fruits and plants grew in the conservatory there?

3. Did you see a rain forest? What is a rain forest? What are the levels of a rain forest?

4. Plant leaves come in many shapes and sizes with various designs and patterns on them. What is the purpose of the designs? What are some functions of plant leaves?

5. What is pollen? List some ways that pollen is carried.

6. Plants need water to live and grow. Predict what would happen if your state suffered a severe drought. Think about plants, animals, and people.

7. After a rain a rainbow can sometimes be seen. List the colors of the rainbow. Name some plants that are those colors.

8. What is a deciduous tree? Explain why leaves change color in the fall. List five deciduous trees found in your state.

9. What is a conifer? What is a common use of a conifer? List five conifer trees. What conifer trees are found in your state?

Activities

1. Draw a map of the world showing the locations of rain forests.

2. Either draw a picture or make a model of a rain forest. You should show the different levels and the vegetation found at each level. Remember to include the animals of the rain forest.

3. Draw a picture of a plant leaf showing the design or pattern on it.

4. Draw a picture of a rainbow, using the correct colors. Remember the pot of gold at the end.

5. Plant a rainbow garden using plants that are the colors of the rainbow.

FIRE STATION

Questions

1. Name the fire department or station that you visited.
2. What is the phone number you should call in an emergency?
3. List five things that can start fires.
4. Why is it important to have a smoke alarm or detector in your home?
5. In addition to a smoke alarm, what other item is good to have in your home in case of a fire?
6. Why is it important to stay close to the floor in a fire?
7. Why should you touch a door before opening it if you are caught in a fire?
8. What does "stop, drop, and roll" mean?
9. Why is it important to have two fire exits from your home?
10. Why is it important to practice fire drills at home and at school?
11. Are ambulances a part of fire department equipment? If they are, explain why.

Activities

1. Draw a fire exit plan for your house.
2. Plan a fire drill schedule for your family at home. Explain the fire exits and drill to your family. Try it and see if it works.
3. Draw pictures that show "stop, drop, and roll."
4. Draw a picture that shows hidden fire hazards in the kitchen. Ask a friend to try to find the hazards in the picture.
5. Make a fire safety brochure for children.

From *Kids on the Go* by John Haberberger • ©1994 • Teacher Ideas Press • P.O. Box 6633 • Englewood, CO 80155-6633

HISTORICAL MUSEUM

Questions

1. Artifacts are used as a source of information about the past. What are artifacts?

2. Native Americans lived throughout the country that became the United States. What Native American nations lived in the area of the country where your state is located?

3. Compare the early school classroom with your own classroom. Show how they are alike and different, using the Venn diagram.

4. What games were played by children who lived at the turn of the century? What toys did they play with?

5. A city begins and grows for different reasons. Think of the city where you live. Why was it started in that place? What things contributed to its growth?

6. What materials were used to build houses at the turn of the century? Compare those early houses with a house of today. Show how they are alike and different, using the Venn diagram.

7. Name five things we have today that did not exist at the turn of the century.

Activities

1. Draw pictures of a boy and a girl dressed in clothes they might have worn in 1900.

2. Learn about a colorful character from your city's past. Share what you learned about this person.

3. Draw a mural or make a diorama showing how your city looked at the turn of the century.

4. Make a timeline showing the important events in your city's growth.

5. Make a list of things you would put in a time capsule that would be opened in 100 years.

6. Make a student handbook for an early school. Your handbook could contain school rules and any other information you think would have been important at the time.

7. Do you think that historical museums are important? Tell why or why not. Predict what might happen if there were no historical museums.

From *Kids on the Go* by John Haberberger • ©1994 • Teacher Ideas Press • P.O. Box 6633 • Englewood, CO 80155-6633

HISTORIC SITE

Questions

1. What is the name of the historic site you visited?

2. What is the oldest structure at the site? How old is it? What is the historical significance of the structure?

3. Electricity was not known in the pioneer days. How did the early settlers light their cabins?

4. Plumbing was not known in the pioneer days. Describe the bathroom the early settlers used. How did they obtain water? What did they call the bathroom?

5. What games did the pioneer children play?

6. What toys did the pioneer children play with? Compare them with the toys of today. Show how they are alike and different, using the Venn diagram.

7. We buy butter at the grocery store. How did the pioneers make butter?

8. Name some of the chores pioneer children performed.

9. Name five things made of wood in the pioneer home.

10. Would you want to have lived in those days? Explain why or why not.

Activities

1. Either draw a picture or make a model of a pioneer cabin. You should include furniture, the bathroom, and a barn.

2. Make a cornhusk doll.

3. Prepare a menu for a pioneer supper or breakfast.

4. Make a dinner bell and use it to call your family to meals.

5. Draw pictures of a pioneer boy and girl dressed in the clothes that they wore in those days.

6. Make butter to share with the class.

7. Many settlers came West looking for gold. What is panning for gold? Demonstrate how this is done.

From *Kids on the Go* by John Haberberger • ©1994 • Teacher Ideas Press • P.O. Box 6633 • Englewood, CO 80155-6633

LAW ENFORCEMENT FACILITY

Questions

1. What are five duties of a police officer?

2. What is the job of an investigator?

3. What is evidence? Evidence is kept in a locked vault. Why is it important to keep evidence secure?

4. Most items that people buy have a serial number stamped on them. Explain the importance of serial numbers. Why should you keep a record of the serial numbers of your things?

5. Describe what occurs in the briefing room.

6. People commit many different crimes. What do you think is the most serious crime? Tell why.

7. The emergency phone number is 911. Why are 911 calls recorded and saved? Name three emergencies that would require an emergency call.

Activities

1. Evidence must be described accurately. Choose an object in your desk, your pocket or purse, your classroom, or your home, and write a one-paragraph description of it. Also draw a picture of it.

2. Make a wanted poster for an evil character in a fairy tale.

3. Draw a picture of a police car. Your picture should include both the inside and outside of the car. If you were designing a police car, can you think of something that would be helpful to have? If you can, add it to your drawing and explain what it is.

4. You are familiar with Superman and the other superheroes. Create a new superhero and write a comic strip that shows the adventures of your hero.

5. Create a new TV show about the police or a criminal investigator. Write a description of your show or character. You could also write a story line for the first episode.

From *Kids on the Go* by John Haberberger • ©1994 • Teacher Ideas Press • P.O. Box 6633 • Englewood, CO 80155-6633

LIBRARY

Questions

1. Name the library that you visited.

2. Books can be fiction or nonfiction. What does *nonfiction* mean?

3. What is your favorite fictional book? Who is the author? What other books has that person written?

4. Nonfiction books are cataloged according to the Dewey decimal system. Who was Dewey? When did he live? Explain what the numbers mean.

5. Reference material usually cannot be checked out. Give three examples of reference material.

6. Explain why poetry is considered nonfiction in the library.

7. Does the library you visited use a computerized checkout system? What are the advantages of using computers?

Activities

1. Design a bookmark.

2. Design a cover for your favorite book.

3. Write a letter to your favorite author.

4. Choose a book and read it to the class.

NATURAL HISTORY MUSEUM

Questions

1. Give the name of the museum you visited.

2. A museum is a display of a collection of objects. If your visit focused on a certain area of interest or topic, tell what it was.

3. Using the first letter of your name, list five objects you saw that begin with that letter.

4. Do you think that natural history museums are important? Explain why or why not.

5. Write about one new thing you learned from your visit to the museum.

6. What was the most interesting thing you saw at the museum?

7. Would you recommend this museum to a friend? Explain why or why not.

8. Predict what might happen if there were no museums of natural history.

Activities

1. Design a T-shirt advertising the museum you visited or an exhibit you saw.

2. Write a letter to your parents telling them about your field trip and what you learned.

3. Make a diorama showing a display you saw.

4. Draw a picture of a display you saw, putting yourself in the picture.

5. Build a model of something you saw at the museum.

6. If you saw an animal exhibit, compare one of the animals with a dog or a cat. Show how they are alike and different, using the Venn diagram.

From *Kids on the Go* by John Haberberger • ©1994 • Teacher Ideas Press • P.O. Box 6633 • Englewood, CO 80155-6633

NEWSPAPER PLANT

Questions

1. What is the name of the newspaper you visited?

2. How many people subscribe to the paper?

3. List the steps in the production of a newspaper.

4. A "full roll" of newsprint weighs about one ton. How many pounds equal one ton? Name something else that weighs a ton.

5. Newsprint waste is recycled. Explain why recycling is important.

6. What is a press run?

7. The newspaper is printed on presses. What is a nine-unit press? What is a ten-unit press?

8. Explain the difference between a straight run and a collect run.

9. What is offset printing? How is it different from using a letter press?

10. Why are special sections of the paper preprinted? What sections of the paper are preprinted? Give some examples.

Activities

1. Compare this newspaper with another paper from your city or state. Show how they are alike and different, using the Venn diagram.

2. Make a scrapbook of the newspaper plant you visited. Your scrapbook could include pictures showing the various steps in the production process and examples of the different sections of the daily or Sunday paper.

3. Is an editorial fact or opinion? Write an editorial on the school lunches served in your school.

4. Demonstrate how the food section could be used in the classroom. Explain what different things children can learn using this section.

5. Create a newspaper for your class or school. What are the different sections of your paper?

STADIUM

Questions

1. What is the name of the stadium you visited?
2. Is the stadium covered or is it open?
3. How many spectators can be seated in the stadium? What is a spectator?
4. Name the different uses of the stadium. What types of sporting events, concerts, and other performances are held there?
5. What does *prohibited* mean? What are some items that are prohibited from being brought into the stadium? Why do you think these items are prohibited?
6. If you visited the locker room, describe what you saw.
7. If you visited the scoreboard control room, describe what you saw.
8. If you visited the press box, describe what you saw.
9. Mile High Stadium in Denver is unique in that the entire east stand section is movable. Does the stadium you visited have any special features? If it does, explain what they are.
10. List three facts you learned about the stadium you visited.

Activities

1. Draw a picture of the stadium you visited.
2. List the different jobs that are required to operate the stadium. If you were offered any one of these jobs, which would you choose? Explain why.
3. What changes would you make to improve the stadium?
4. Name the team or teams that use the stadium. Design a new jersey for them.
5. Draw an unusual picture to be flashed on the scoreboard.
6. Build a model of the stadium you visited.

From *Kids on the Go* by John Haberberger • ©1994 • Teacher Ideas Press • P.O. Box 6633 • Englewood, CO 80155-6633

TRANSPORTATION MUSEUM

Questions

1. Name the museum you visited.
2. What different forms of transportation did you see there?
3. What is a "horseless carriage?"
4. A Stanley Steamer was a steam-driven car. Explain how steam is used to power a car.
5. What fuels were used to power the early automobiles? What fuels are used now?
6. Explain how an electric car works. What is the source of the electricity?
7. List five brand names of early cars. How did REO get its name?
8. Early bicycles had wooden frames. What materials are used for bicycle frames today?
9. What was the oldest thing you saw at the museum? In what year was it made? How old is it now?
10. Which car in the museum would you most like to have for your own? Why?

Activities

1. Compare an early automobile with a present-day auto. Show how they are alike and different, using the Venn diagram.
2. You are asked to create a new economical, nonpolluting fuel for cars of the future. Use your knowledge and imagination to invent this fuel. Explain what it is and how it works.
3. Build models of an early-day automobile and a present-day car.
4. What will the car of the future look like? Draw a picture of your idea of tomorrow's car.
5. Pretend that you are taking a bicycle tour of the United States. You will spend three months riding around the country. You will be on your bike for long hours each day. Create a special bicycle for the tour—a dream machine. Draw a picture of your creation and label the different things you put on your bicycle.
5. Brainstorm with a friend and list all the ways you can think of to get from one place to another.
6. Draw a picture of the most unusual thing you saw at the museum.

From *Kids on the Go* by John Haberberger • ©1994 • Teacher Ideas Press • P.O. Box 6633 • Englewood, CO 80155-6633

APPENDIX A

Alabama

Capital: Montgomery
Statehood: December 14, 1819 (22nd state)
Nicknames: Cotton State; Yellowhammer State; Heart of Dixie
Motto: "We Dare Defend Our Rights"
Horse: Rocking Horse
Flower: Camellia
Bird: Yellowhammer
Insect: Monarch Butterfly

Alaska

Capital: Juneau
Statehood: January 3, 1959 (49th state)
Nicknames: Last Frontier; Land of the Midnight Sun; Great Fun Land
Motto: "North to the Future"
Flower: Forget-me-not
Bird: Willow Ptarmigan
Fish: King Salmon
Fossil: Woolly Mammoth
Sport: Dog Mushing

Arizona

Capital: Phoenix
Statehood: February 14, 1912 (48th state)
Nickname: Grand Canyon State
Motto: "God Enriches"
Flower: Blossom of the Saguaro Cactus
Bird: Cactus Wren
Official Neckwear: Bola Tie

Arkansas

Capital: Little Rock
Statehood: June 15, 1836 (25th state)
Nicknames: Land of Opportunity, and the Natural State
Motto: "The People Rule"
Flower: Apple Blossom
Bird: Mockingbird
Insect: Honeybee
Musical Instrument: Fiddle
Beverage: Milk

California

Capital: Sacramento
Statehood: September 9, 1850 (31st state)
Nickname: Golden State
Motto: "I Have Found It"
Animal: California Grizzly Bear
Flower: Golden Poppy
Bird: California Valley Quail
Fossil: Saber-Toothed Cat
Marine Mammal: California Gray Whale

Colorado

Capital: Denver
Statehood: August 1, 1876 (38th state)
Nickname: Centennial State
Motto: "Nothing Without Providence"
Animal: Bighorn Sheep
Flower: Columbine
Bird: Lark Bunting
Fossil: Stegosaurus

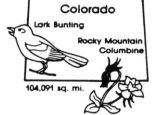

Connecticut

Capital: Hartford
Statehood: January 9, 1788 (5th state)
Nickname: Constitution State; Nutmeg State
Motto: "He Who Transplanted Still Sustains"
Animal: Sperm Whale
Flower: Mountain Laurel
Bird: American Robin
Insect: European "Praying" Mantis
Ship: *USS Nautilus*

Delaware

Capital: Dover
Statehood: December 7, 1787 (1st state)
Nicknames: First State; Diamond State
Motto: "Liberty and Independence"
Flower: Peach Blossom
Bird: Blue Hen Chicken
Beverage: Milk

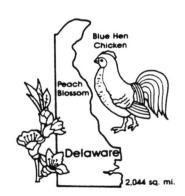

Florida

Capital: Tallahassee
Statehood: March 3, 1845 (27th state)
Nickname: Sunshine State
Motto: "In God We Trust"
Animal: Florida Panther
Flower: Orange Blossom
Bird: Mockingbird
Marine Mammal: Manatee
Saltwater Mammal: Porpoise
Shell: Horse Conch

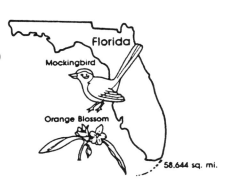

Georgia

Capital: Atlanta
Statehood: January 2, 1788 (4th state)
Nicknames: Peach State; Empire State of the South
Motto: "Wisdom, Justice, and Moderation"
Flower: Cherokee Rose
Bird: Brown Thrasher
Butterfly: Tiger Swallowtail
Insect: Honeybee
Fish: Largemouth Bass

Hawaii

Capital: Honolulu
Statehood: August 21, 1959 (50th state)
Nickname: Aloha State
Motto: "The Life of the Land Is Perpetuated in Righteousness"
Flower: Hibiscus
Bird: Hawaiian Goose
Tree: Kukui Tree (Candlenut)

Idaho

Capital: Boise
Statehood: July 3, 1890 (43rd state)
Nickname: Gem State
Motto: "It Is Forever"
Flower: Syringa
Bird: Mountain Bluebird
Horse: Appaloosa

Illinois

Capital: Springfield
Statehood: December 3, 1818 (21st state)
Nicknames: Land of Lincoln; Prairie State
Motto: "State Sovereignty, National Union"
Animal: White-tailed Deer
Flower: Native Violet
Bird: Cardinal
Fish: Bluegill

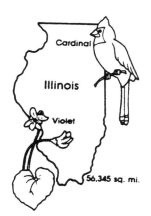

Indiana

Capital: Indianapolis
Statehood: December 11, 1816 (19th state)
Nickname: Hoosier State
Motto: "Crossroads of America"
Flower: Peony
Bird: Cardinal
Poem: "Indiana" by Arthur Franklin Mapes

Iowa

Capital: Des Moines
Statehood: December 28, 1846 (29th state)
Nickname: Hawkeye State
Motto: "Our Liberties We Prize and Our Rights We Will Maintain"
Flower: Wild Rose
Bird: Eastern Goldfinch

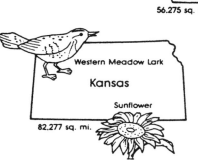

Kansas

Capital: Topeka
Statehood: January 29, 1861 (34th state)
Nickname: Sunflower State
Motto: "To the Stars Through Difficulties"
Animal: American Buffalo
Flower: Wild Native Sunflower
Bird: Western Meadowlark
Reptile: Ornate Box Turtle

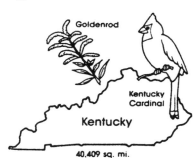

Kentucky

Capital: Frankfort
Statehood: June 1, 1792 (15th state)
Nickname: Bluegrass State
Motto: "United We Stand, Divided We Fall"
Animal: Gray Squirrel
Flower: Goldenrod
Bird: Cardinal
Fossil: Brachiopod
Fish: Kentucky Bass

Louisiana

Capital: Baton Rouge
Statehood: April 30, 1812 (18th state)
Nickname: Pelican State
Motto: "Union, Justice, and Confidence"
Flower: Magnolia
Bird: Eastern Brown Pelican
Crustacean: Crawfish
Dog: Catahoula Leopard Dog

Maine

Capital: Augusta
Statehood: March 15, 1820 (23rd state)
Nickname: Pine Tree State
Motto: "I Direct"
Animal: Moose
Flower: White Pine Cone and Tassel
Bird: Chickadee
Fish: Landlocked Salmon
Cat: Maine Coon Cat

Maryland

Capital: Annapolis
Statehood: April 28, 1788 (7th state)
Nicknames: Old Line State; Free State
Motto: "Manly Deeds, Womanly Words"
Flower: Black-eyed Susan
Bird: Baltimore Oriole
Dog: Chesapeake Bay Retriever
Fish: Striped Bass
Boat: Skipjack
Sport: Jousting

Massachusetts

Capital: Boston
Statehood: February 6, 1788 (6th state)
Nickname: Bay State
Motto: "By the Sword We Seek Peace, But Only
    Peace Under Liberty"
Animal: Morgan Horse
Flower: Mayflower
Bird: Chickadee
Dog: Boston Terrier
Beverage: Cranberry Juice
Historical Rock: Plymouth Rock

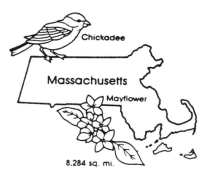

Michigan

Capital: Lansing
Statehood: January 26, 1837 (26th state)
Nickname: Wolverine State
Motto: "If You Seek a Pleasant Peninsula, Look Around You"
Flower: Apple Blossom
Bird: Robin
Fish: Brook Trout

Minnesota

Capital: St. Paul
Statehood: May 11, 1858 (32nd state)
Nickname: Gopher State
Motto: "The Star of the North"
Flower: Pink and White Lady's Slipper
Bird: Common Loon
Fish: Walleye
Grain: Wild Rice
Mushroom: Morel

Mississippi

Capital: Jackson
Statehood: December 10, 1817 (20th state)
Nickname: Magnolia State
Motto: "By Valor and Arms"
Animal: White-tailed Deer
Flower: Magnolia
Bird: Mockingbird
Water Mammal: Bottlenosed Dolphin
Fish: Black Bass
Beverage: Milk

Missouri

Capital: Jefferson City
Statehood: August 10, 1821 (24th state)
Nickname: Show Me State
Motto: "Let the Welfare of the People Be the Supreme Law"
Flower: White Hawthorn
Bird: Bluebird
Insect: Honeybee
Fossil: Crinoid

Montana

Capital: Helena
Statehood: November 8, 1889 (41st state)
Nickname: Treasure State
Motto: "Gold and Silver"
Animal: Grizzly Bear
Flower: Bitterroot
Bird: Western Meadowlark
State Ballad: "Montana Melody"
Fossil: Duck-billed Dinosaur

Nebraska

Capital: Lincoln
Statehood: March 1, 1867 (37th state)
Nickname: Cornhusker State
Motto: "Equality Before the Law"
Animal: White-tailed Deer
Flower: Goldenrod
Bird: Western Meadowlark
Insect: Honeybee

Nevada

Capital: Carson City
Statehood: October 31, 1864 (36th state)
Nicknames: Silver State; Sagebrush State
Motto: "All for Our Country"
Animal: Desert Bighorn Sheep
Flower: Sagebrush
Bird: Mountain Bluebird
Fish: Cutthroat Trout
Fossil: Ichthyosaur

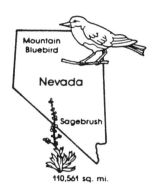

New Hampshire

Capital: Concord
Statehood: June 21, 1788 (9th state)
Nickname: Granite State
Motto: "Live Free or Die"
Animal: White-tailed Deer
Flower: Purple Lilac
Bird: Purple Finch
Insect: Ladybug

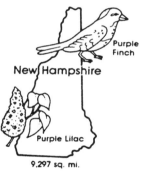

New Jersey

Capital: Trenton
Statehood: December 18, 1787 (3rd state)
Nickname: Garden State
Motto: "Liberty and Prosperity"
Animal: Horse
Flower: Violet
Bird: Eastern Goldfinch
Insect: Honeybee

New Mexico

    Capital: Santa Fe
    Statehood: January 6, 1912 (47th state)
    Nickname: Land of Enchantment
    Motto: "It Grows as It Goes"
    Animal: Black Bear
    Flower: Yucca (Our Lord's Candles)
    Bird: Chaparral Bird
    Fossil: Coelophysis
    Vegetable: Pinto Bean and the Chili

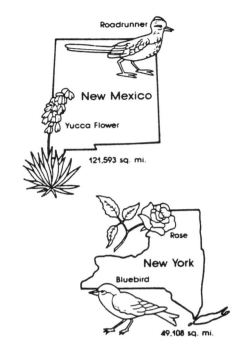

New York

    Capital: Albany
    Statehood: July 26, 1788 (11th state)
    Nickname: Empire State
    Motto: "Ever Upward"
    Animal: American Beaver
    Flower: Rose
    Bird: Bluebird
    Fossil: Eurypterus Remipes

North Carolina

    Capital: Raleigh
    Statehood: November 21, 1789 (12th state)
    Nickname: Tar Heel
    Motto: "To Be, Rather Than to Seem"
    Flower: Dogwood
    Bird: Cardinal
    Mammal: Grey Squirrel
    Dog: Plott Hound
    Beverage: Milk

North Dakota

    Capital: Bismarck
    Statehood: November 2, 1889 (39th state)
    Nicknames: Flickertail State; Sioux State
    Motto: "Liberty and Union, Now and Forever, One and Inseparable"
    Flower: Wild Prairie Rose
    Bird: Western Meadowlark
    March: "Spirit of the Land"
    Stone: Teredo Petrified Wood
    Fish: Northern Pike

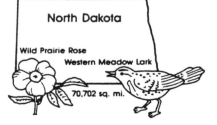

Ohio

Capital: Columbus
Statehood: March 1, 1803 (17th state)
Nickname: Buckeye State
Motto: "With God, All Things Are Possible"
Animal: White-tailed Deer
Flower: Scarlet Carnation
Bird: Cardinal
Stone: Ohio Flint
Insect: Ladybug

Oklahoma

Capital: Oklahoma City
Statehood: November 16, 1907 (46th state)
Nickname: Sooner State
Motto: "Labor Conquers All Things"
Animal: American Buffalo
Flower: Mistletoe
Bird: Scissor-tailed Flycatcher
Grass: Indian Grass
Reptile: Collared Lizard

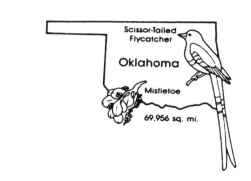

Oregon

Capital: Salem
Statehood: February 14, 1859 (33rd state)
Nickname: Beaver State
Motto: "The Union"
Animal: American Beaver
Flower: Oregon Grape
Bird: Western Meadowlark
Insect: Oregon Swallowtail Butterfly

Pennsylvania

Capital: Harrisburg
Statehood: December 12, 1787 (2nd state)
Nickname: Keystone State
Motto: "Virtue, Liberty, and Independence"
Animal: White-tailed Deer
Flower: Mountain Laurel
Game Bird: Ruffed Grouse
Insect: Firefly
Dog: Great Dane

Rhode Island

Capital: Providence
Statehood: May 29, 1790 (13th state)
Nickname: Little Rhody
Motto: "Hope"
Animal: Quahaug
Flower: Violet
Bird: Rhode Island Red

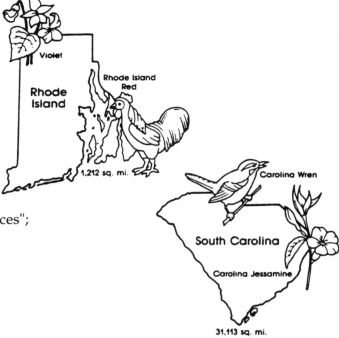

South Carolina

Capital: Columbia
Statehood: May 23, 1788 (8th state)
Nickname: Palmetto State
Motto: "Prepared in Mind and Resources";
    "While I Breathe, I Hope"
Animal: White-tailed Deer
Flower: Yellow Jessamine
Bird: Carolina Wren
Fish: Striped Bass
Dance: Shag

South Dakota

Capital: Pierre
Statehood: November 2, 1889 (40th state)
Nicknames: Sunshine State; Coyote State
Motto: "Under God the People Rule"
Animal: Coyote
Flower: American Pasqueflower
Bird: Ringnecked Pheasant
Fish: Walleye
Insect: Honeybee
Grass: Western Wheat Grass

Tennessee

Capital: Nashville
Statehood: June 1, 1796 (16th state)
Nicknames: Volunteer State; Big Bend State
Motto: "Agriculture and Commerce"
Animal: Raccoon
Flower: Iris
Bird: Mockingbird
Wildflower: Passion Flower

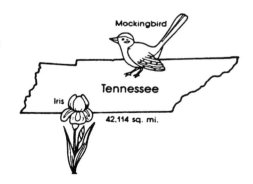

Texas

Capital: Austin
Statehood: December 29, 1845 (28th state)
Nickname: Lone Star State
Motto: "Friendship"
Flower: Bluebonnet
Bird: Mockingbird
Stone: Petrified Palmwood
Dish: Chili
Seashell: Lightning Whelk

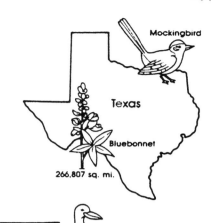

Utah

Capital: Salt Lake City
Statehood: January 4, 1896 (45th state)
Nickname: Beehive State
Motto: "Industry"
Animal: Rocky Mountain Elk
Flower: Sego Lily
Bird: California Seagull
Fish: Rainbow Trout
Insect: Honeybee

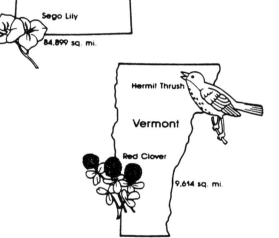

Vermont

Capital: Montpelier
Statehood: March 4, 1791 (14th state)
Nickname: Green Mountain State
Motto: "Freedom and Unity"
Animal: Morgan Horse
Flower: Red Clover
Bird: Hermit Thrush
Insect: Honeybee
Beverage: Milk

Virginia

Capital: Richmond
Statehood: June 25, 1788 (10th state)
Nicknames: Old Dominion; Mother of Presidents
Motto: "Thus Always to Tyrants"
Animal: American Foxhound
Flower: Dogwood
Bird: Cardinal
Shell: Oyster
Beverage: Milk

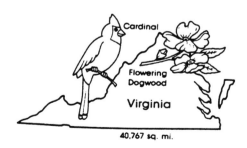

Washington

Capital: Olympia
Statehood: November 11, 1889 (42nd state)
Nicknames: Evergreen State; Chinook State
Motto: "By and By"
Flower: Western Rhododendron
Bird: Willow Goldfinch
Dance: Square Dance
Fish: Steelhead Trout

Washington. DC

Became the U.S. Capital: December 1, 1800
Motto: "Justice to All"
Flower: American Beauty Rose
Bird: Wood Thrush
Tree: Scarlet Oak

West Virginia

Capital: Charleston
Statehood: June 20, 1863 (35th state)
Nicknames: Mountain State; Panhandle State
Motto: "Mountaineers Are Always Free"
Animal: Black Bear
Flower: Big Laurel
Bird: Cardinal
Fruit: Apple
Fish: Brook Trout

Wisconsin

Capital: Madison
Statehood: May 29, 1848 (30th state)
Nickname: Badger State
Motto: "Forward"
Animal: Badger
Flower: Wood Violet
Bird: Robin
Fish: Muskellunge
Insect: Honeybee

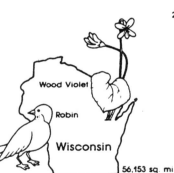

Wyoming

Capital: Cheyenne
Statehood: July 10, 1890 (44th state)
Nicknames: Equality State; Cowboy State
Motto: "Equal Rights"
Animal: Bison
Flower: Indian Paintbrush
Bird: Western Meadowlark
Song: "Wyoming"

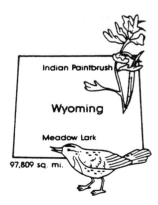

Appendix B

Venn Diagram

compare

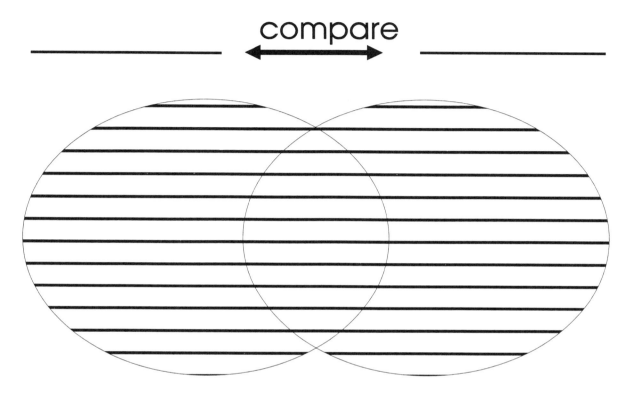

Where the two circles overlap is where the items are alike. The outer circles show how the items are different.

From *Kids on the Go* by John Haberberger • ©1994 • Teacher Ideas Press • P.O. Box 6633 • Englewood, CO 80155-6633

BIBLIOGRAPHY

Kane, Robert S. *Hawaii at Its Best*. Lincolnwood, Ill: NTC Publishing Group, 1989.

Milepost (Spring 1992-Spring 1993). Bothell, Wash.: GTE Discovery Publications, 1992.

Mobil Travel Guide: Great Lakes. New York: Prentice Hall, 1992.

Mobil Travel Guide: Middle Atlantic. New York: Prentice Hall, 1992.

Mobil Travel Guide: Northeast. New York: Prentice Hall, 1992.

Mobil Travel Guide: Northwest and Great Plains. New York: Prentice Hall, 1991.

Mobil Travel Guide: Southeast. New York: Prentice Hall, 1992.

Mobil Travel Guide: Southwest and South Central. New York: Prentice Hall, 1992.

Mobil Travel Guide: California and the West. New York: Prentice Hall, 1992.

About the Author

John Haberberger was born and raised in Seattle, Washington. He did his undergraduate work at the Oregon College of Education. He has a master's degree in Early Childhood Education from the University of Colorado and has completed doctoral work in Educational Administration at the University of Colorado.

John currently lives in Littleton, Colorado and is an elementary school teacher for Jefferson County School District. He has been teaching for twenty-one years. He was recognized as a "Teacher Who Makes a Difference" by the Rocky Mountain News and Channel 4 in Denver. He has coached Odyssey of the Mind teams for a number of years, winning a district competition and placing well in a state competition.